Review of Research Trends and an Annotated Bibliography:

Social and Economic Consequences of the Arms Race and of Disarmament

unesco

ISBN 92-3-101552-4
French edition 92-3-201552-8
Spanish edition 92-3-301552-1

Published in 1978 by the
United Nations Educational,
Scientific and Cultural Organization
7, Place de Fontenoy, 75700 Paris, France

Composed and printed in the workshops
of Unesco

Printed in France

Preface

For several decades Unesco has been assisting its Member States and the academic community in developing peace research. Among the priority areas for such research the study of the social and economic aspects of the arms race and disarmament has been given particular attention. It may be noted in this regard that the General Conference of Unesco, at its nineteenth session, observed "that a serious obstacle to the strengthening of peace is constituted by the continuing arms race, which absorbs billions of dollars, places a terrible burden on the economy of States, prevents enormous sums from being used for peaceful, constructive purposes, adversely affects the struggle of peoples for their national and social emancipation, and hinders the solving of many socio-economic problems".

Much of the vast amount of material published on the social and economic aspects of disarmament is not easily available in many parts of the world. To assist researchers, students and officials, particularly in areas where libraries may not be very complete, Unesco decided to prepare the present report and bibliography for its "Reports and Papers in the Social Sciences" series.

The bibliography has been compiled for Unesco under the auspices of the International Peace Research Association (IPRA), by the International Institute for Peace (Vienna), the Arbeitsgruppe Rüstung und Unterentwicklung (Hamburg)

and the Tampere Peace Research Institute (Tampere), concentrating respectively on publications from the socialist countries, the Third World and market-economy countries. The IPRA secretariat was solely responsible for decisions regarding items to be included in the bibliography.

The review of research trends in the study of social and economic consequences of the arms race and of disarmament was written by Peter Lock and Herbert Wulf from the Arbeitsgruppe Rüstung und Unterentwicklung (Section 3 and Annexes I and II), by Alexander Kalyadin from the Institute of World Economy and International Relations in Moscow (Section 4) and by Raimo Väyrynen from the International Peace Research Association and Tampere Peace Research Institute (Section 2).

Unesco extends its warmest thanks to the General Editor, Raimo Väyrynen, Secretary-General, and to the International Peace Research Association for their invaluable co-operation in preparing this bibliography; and to the institutes and scholars who co-operated with the Association on this project.

The selection of items for inclusion in the bibliography and the opinions expressed do not necessarily represent the views of Unesco.

Designations used do not imply the expression of any opinion whatsoever concerning the legal status of any country or territory, or of the authorities of any country or territory.

Contents

A review of research trends in the study of the social and economic consequences of the arms race and of disarmament

1. GENERAL BACKGROUND

The ending of the arms race and the achieving of disarmament are priority problems of our time. The world public is expressing deep concern over the continuing arms race and its negative social and economic consequences.

For this reason it is only natural that the impact of the arms race and the consequences, problems and tasks which might be caused by measures taken to achieve disarmament, have been the subject of many special studies done both in the West and in the East by individual scholars, groups of experts and large scientific teams. Official reports of United Nations experts deserve special mention.

Today the social and economic problems of disarmament assume special topicality. We have in mind not only the increased material resources annually used for non-productive aims, but also the growing acuteness of food, raw material and energy problems, the aggravation of the world ecological situation, the unsatisfied social and economic needs of the majority of the world population, the prospects of development of new, more formidable types of mass destruction weapons, etc. On the other hand, encouraging prospects have opened up in connection with the development of the process of détente, which has already led to considerable changes in the entire system of international relations. Within the process of the deepening of détente new opportunities appear for arriving at agreements limiting armaments and leading to disarmament.

Serious consideration is given in this bibliography to problems of stopping the nuclear arms race, nuclear disarmament, the limitation of the use of science for military purposes and particularly the banning of the development of new weapons of mass destruction, regional measures of military détente, the reduction of conventional armaments, armed forces and military budgets, and so on. The treatment of these problems reflects conviction in the necessity of carrying out effective disarmament measures.

At the same time the arms race has continued in an unabated manner, and the efforts to reverse the trend, although numerous, have not so far been very effective. The question is of a long process towards disarmament containing both dangers and promises. Serious attention should be also given to the militarization of the Third World, which has manifested itself especially during the last ten years in increasing arms transfers from the centre nations, in efforts to build domestic arms production in some countries as well as in local arms races, e.g. in Latin America, the Middle East and the Indian subcontinent. There have been far fewer efforts to curb these tendencies towards higher levels of armament than in East-West relations in which there is already a web of agreements and negotiations which aim at stabilizing the military situation and lessening the risk of nuclear war. Although there are many good reasons for proposing that increasing attention should be devoted to arms transfers and arms production in the Third World one must, nevertheless, bear in mind that the bulk of military spending takes place in the industrialized part of the world, which also controls the most destructive types of weapons. On the other hand, the present danger of the proliferation of nuclear weapons in the Third World, although still in its infancy, may change the situation quite drastically. It may not be exaggerated to maintain that nuclear proliferation is one of the most serious dangers to international peace and security.

Research on various aspects of the arms race is never an easy task because of paucity of available information. This is largely due to deep-rooted military secrecy which is thought to be necessary for the maintenance of national security. It has been widely admitted that emphasis on military secrecy has resulted in exaggerations and distortions which were hardly possible in other fields of social life. This comment is especially pertinent in the case of research on the development of military technology in general and individual weapon systems in particular, which in practice means that investigations concerning arms manufacturing and military R&D (Research and Development) are particularly hampered by the secrecy. The problem of secrecy is not equally urgent in the study of social and economic consequences of the arms race and disarmament, although its implications can easily be conceived of there as well.

In this particular research a greater problem may be the inherent complexity of the analysis which requires the integration of military, economic, sociological and political perspectives. As statistics on arms production and exports, military R&D, military manpower, etc., are seldom available in processed form - contrary to the practice prevailing in other sectors of the economy - a lot of imagination and unconventional methodological solutions are needed if a researcher really wants to penetrate into the essence of consequences of the arms race and disarmament. In other words, implementation of comprehensive research tasks may lead to the reduction of methodological stringency, traditionally defined; the best is often an enemy of the good.

2. CONSEQUENCES OF THE ARMS RACE AND OF DISARMAMENT

The question of the arms race and disarmament has long been formulated in strategic terms. Naturally the consequences of wars and of arms races on population and national economy were of some interest to the scholars concerned, but in the early sixties a more profound interest in social and economic aspects started to develop. It must be emphasized, however, that these studies were devoted to national problems, and they seldom considered the international implications. Furthermore, they were predominantly cross-sectional by nature and consequently did not very often consider the historical development which had led to the situation at hand.

The scope and significance of the economic aspects of disarmament are intimately linked with and determined by the economic effects of the arms race. That is why it is necessary to take a brief look at some aspects of armament policies. The experience of several decades past has shown that the development of war technology leads to a situation in which the war potential of individual nations increasingly depends on their general economic potential, including the level of development of scientific research and the possibility of applying its results. This is particularly evident in the present armaments race which, in effect, constitutes a form of competition of national economies in the production of new and ever more destructive weapons. Recently, however, transnational collaboration has considerably increased in the production of arms and other military equipment, especially in the North Atlantic region.

Owing to the high level of development of war technology, the military expenditure necessary for modern armies imposes a substantial burden on national economies. This burden is further increased because of rapid change in military technology, leading to a comparatively early obsolescense of weapons and calling for additional increased investment in the production of new models of weapons and military equipment.(1) Recently the share of military spending of the national product has decreased in most countries, but the technological development of armaments has effects that are mostly felt in technologically advanced sectors of national economies.

2.1 Effects of the arms race

Effects of the arms race can be divided into several subcategories. An indispensable correlate of the arms race is the emergence of military-industrial complexes (MIC) with considerable power in society. Extensive literature dealing with the MICs was to a large extent a counter-reaction to earlier Western literature that had devoted scant attention to the structural preconditions and consequences of the armaments race, and was by character rather individualizing. This literature may have had its roots in inter-war research and pamphlets on the operations of defence firms and on arms deals: "the bloody armaments international" and the "merchants of death" tradition. Only after the early 1960s did the MIC literature start to flourish, probably as a consequence of the increased role of these complexes in various countries, behind their armaments policies.

The analysis of MICs has proliferated in several directions, with two major interpretations, élitist and pluralist. (2) According to the élitist interpretation, the MIC is a fairly tightly co-ordinated "power élite" fully capable of shaping the course of the arms race according to its own interests. The critics of this approach have claimed that it attributes too much omnipotence to the complex which is not, after all, so determining a factor in the conduct of armament policies; the MIC can also fail. In the pluralist view, the MIC is a loosely co-ordinated group of actors with some common interests and who consequently work for the same type of policies, but whose components also form a countervailing power to each other. The MIC approach is in any case connected with the increasing role given to domestic factors in arms race research.

The heyday of MIC analysis can be placed in the late 1960s and the early 1970s. Nowadays its relative significance is declining, partly as a consequence of criticism directed at the approach. Criticism is of two main types, both focusing on the scientific inadequacy of the MIC theory, although from different premises. Slater and Nardin argue that the weaknesses of the theory are the following: (1) reliance on a theory of conspiracy as the basis of causal inference, (2) simplistic economic determinism, (3) inconsistent specification of the supposed membership of the MIC, and (4) implausible assumptions about the nature, scope and type of power ascribed to the complex.(3) Egbert Jahn, on the other hand, has pointed out that the MIC conception is a variant of the liberal interest-group theory and especially of its élite-theory version, which accords a place of importance to specific small groups in the process of social valorization (Wertrealisierung), Jahn himself seems to favour the analysis of the MIC in close connection with the totality of socio-economic relations of society.(4)

Literature on the MICs has, naturally enough, many shades. Authors tend to place varying degrees of emphasis on the bureaucratic, technological, economic and military components of the complex. The analysis of economic, technolgical and military aspects has apparently been predominant. Hence the impact of the MICs as well as the strategic environment during the Cold War era on public opinion and the intellectual climate has not been analysed to any great extent (though there are some exceptions).(5)

The international dimension of the MICs has not been submitted to any closer scrutiny either. There are, however, some exceptions. Certain authors have recently investigated the transnationalization of the armaments industry through collaborative agreements and direct foreign investments in the military sector of other countries.(6) Jonathan Galloway, for example, has shown that the top United States defence contractors have significant assets in foreign countries and that the top United States based transnational corporations are also among the top defence contractors. In other words, "the giant forms of the economy are apt to be both major defence contractors and world-wide companies".(7) Apart from some fairly narrow empirical studies, however, there is a lack of general theoretical and empirically-oriented investigation on the impact of the arms race and of overall militarization on the international system and its division of labour.

Another mainstream in research on the consequences of the arms race on national societies has been the analysis of relationships between the military establishment and the rest of society, mostly in sociological terms. This tradition has used the military establishment as the focus for analysis and has then studied how its impact has radiated to other social factors and to other sectors of the society. These types of investigations have been concerned, for instance, with the role of the military in relation to total manpower and the role of military research and education, and military values in their corresponding societal contexts. The impact of the military on national political institutions has frequently been studied. This sort of research is no doubt needed to complement the somewhat deterministic picture provided by the

analysis of MICs, to illustrate various non-economic military mechanisms impinging on society. There may, however, be a problem of orientation similar to that in studies dealing with MICs, namely, that the military subsystem is explored too conspicuously in terms of its bilateral relations with other societal subsystems, without paying due attention to wider socio-political contexts.

It is obvious that even at relatively low levels of military spending, economic and social structures - including relations between various social forces and their position in the social structures - are considerably changed under the influence of the military establishment and the military industry. This not only holds true in the case of national societies, but can clearly be seen also internationally.

What is the impact of the arms race on the rate of economic growth? There are some quite different answers. Emile Benoit has shown that the average military burden in developing countries is positively correlated with the rate of economic growth, i.e. military spending tends to foster growth in the economy and vice versa. Benoit admits, however, that there are exceptions such as, Mexico and the United Arab Republic. Deutenmüller has argued that in the Federal Republic of Germany military spending has promoted growth, while Gottheil in his study of the Middle East, and Boulding and Gleason in their analysis of the Japanese case, arrive at the opposite conclusion (in the Japanese case especially in the context of the post-war period).(8)

It is not very easy to provide unequivocal conclusions about the relationship between military spending and economic growth. In some cases, the military industry and establishment may be spearheads of modernization and growth, while in others the situation may be quite the opposite. Thus, the conclusions are probably dependent on the type of country concerned; effects of military spending on economic growth are likely to differ from one sort of political and economic structure to another. Important research is also done on the effects of military spending and arms transfers on the structure of the economy. It is self-evident that military spending, which has some features distinct from other types of public spending, tends to transform the economic structure of countries, although the effects of this transformation are no doubt different in developed and underdeveloped nations. Nowadays it is increasingly claimed that the theory of development must be extended to comprise the role of the military, the production of military hardware and transfers of the latter because, since the colonial period, they have had a definite impact on the political and economic development of underdeveloped countries.(9) This means most obviously that the questions of development must also be separated in this context from considerations of economic growth alone.

We shall later discuss the relationship between development and growth on the one hand and military spending on the other, in terms of opportunity costs, inflation and balance-of-payment problems. Here, it may suffice to say that the question is, after all, one of allocating scarce financial, natural and human resources. Military expenditure pre-empts resources that might otherwise have been invested in technology, capital infrastructure, and in the development of human beings, their skills and innovative capacity for civilian purposes, on which the quality as well as the rate of economic development depend. There are studies showing a close relationship between high rates of military spending and low rates of investment which, in turn, correlate with low growth and productivity gains.(10) Thus high levels of military spending not only distort the structure of the national economy, but also tend to retard economic growth, particularly in industrialized countries. In some underdeveloped countries the situation may be different because high rates of investment result in a kind of forced growth, which, however, is only illusory from the standpoint of the masses.

The interaction between resources allocated to civilian and military purposes can be analysed to a certain degree through a related, although theoretically distinct approach: the analysis of opportunity costs of military spending. This attempts to explain how military expenditure has affected government or private spending in various civilian sectors of the economy, and how these resources could be used alternatively. In contrast to the regional or geographical orientation of the input-output analysts (see below), the opportunity-costs approach is interested in the functional and nation-wide consequences of the arms race and disarmament, and even in implications for the international division of labour.(11) Studies carried out so far seem to indicate that military spending has adverse effects on health and education expenditure as well as on private consumption, but that these effects vary greatly between nations with different economic and political systems.

Empirical investigation has shown that opportunity costs exist in all nations and have generally been stable from 1950 through 1972. The magnitude of the impact, however, is weaker than that observed in some other studies, and the level of economic development had no crucial influence on the extent of opportunity costs. The type of regime is a determining factor in this respect, opportunity costs being greater in "personalist" than in "centrist" or "polyarchic" political systems. It is interesting to note that in recent years centrist regimes have lowered their opportunity costs for military spending in favour of education and health, while polyarchic regimes have been increasing theirs.(12)

High levels of military spending tend to produce social and economic dislocations in national economies. It has been shown, for example, that military spending tends to result in increased inflation rates which, in turn, benefit better-off social strata and deprive underprivileged people.(13) Extensive military expenditure also distorts economic activities by favouring production which does not lead to further productive activities and builds up pressure on prices. This in turn, is a background factor of inflationary tendencies. It is more serious still that military spending allocates resources for purposes which prevent the fulfilment of the most basic needs of citizens. These needs are usually guaranteed to those who serve in the military, but are not always extended to those living in the social periphery.

In developing countries and also in smaller developed countries, the military industry, if it exists at all, seldom produces exportable goods. On the contrary, they import military hardware, causing balance-of-payment problems with all their negative consequences.(14) The same factor also tends to worsen the debt burden in these countries. All in all, in some cases high levels of military spending may provide a catalyst for economic growth, but even then there is no real development, but rather growth fostered by further integration of the society into the centres of international power and by the emergence of the enclave economies. Thus, military spending can hardly anywhere lead to development in the full sense of the word.

A new feature in analysing the impact of the arms race is a world-wide perspective on the uses of natural resources and other environmental consequences of armed forces and their operations. Investigations show that the military establishments, especially in countries with high levels of military spending, are conspicuous consumers of some vital minerals as well as oil, i.e. that they are using up non-renewable resources.(15) In relation to the environmental impact of warfare, the lessons of Viet Nam strongly suggest that modern military technology is especially destructive, not only of human beings, but also of soil, forests and crops and other elements of the environment.(16)

2.2 Consequences of disarmament

The analysis of the consequences of the arms race must logically be accompanied by a consideration of the consequences of potential disarmament. This type of analysis has focused mostly on what might happen in the disarmed alternative which, in turn, is strongly conditioned by the existing quantity and quality of armament levels, measured both in absolute and proportional terms. The first manifestation of interest in this question was the publication of a relatively large number of case studies on the effects of potential disarmament on local communities and regions; different industries were also considered. These studies were normally carried out by the input-output method originally developed by Vassily Leontief.

A feature of these studies was a belief in the usefulness of quantitative models and methods in disarmament research as a means of advancing disarmament: detailed data on the national and regional impacts of military spending would pave the way to disarmament. Another feature was a certain optimism, only partially founded on research results, that disarmament could take place without serious adverse effects on regional and national economies. These studies sometimes contained specific proposals regarding conversion strategies. Foreign aid was often combined with the analysis of the cutbacks on military spending as a possible outlet for resources saved through disarmament.(17) The idea of using the disarmament dividend which, with the proposal to reduce the military budgets of the major military powers, gained new support in the 1970s can, it seems, be traced back to this research tradition.

The impact of disarmament measures has usually been considered from the conversion perspective which, in turn, is connected with the problem of opportunity costs. The possibilities of converting resources used for military purposes to civilian uses has been analysed, not only by the input-output method, but also in case studies on either specific industries strongly dependent on military contracts, or communities affected by such events as the closure of military bases. Most empirical analyses and statements by groups of experts conclude that disarmament is an economically feasible option also in the market economy countries; the doctrine that military spending is necessary for the growth, stability and continued functioning of these economies gains no strong support nowadays. The United Nations Report on the Economic and Social Consequences of Disarmament submitted to the General Assembly in 1962, for example, concluded that "all the problems and difficulties of transition connected with disarmament could be met by appropriate national and international measures. There should thus be no doubt that the diversion to peaceful purposes of the resources now in military use could be accomplished to the benefit of all countries and lead to the improvement of world economic and social conditions. The achievement of general and complete disarmament would be an unqualified blessing to all mankind".(18) Thus, the conversion of resources used for military purposes is believed to be a feasible option, although some reservations to this generalization have been made.

There are several examples of the conversion process not working in certain firms, mostly United States based, which are very dependent on military production - especially aircraft companies which have attempted the transition to civilian production.(19) This underlines the need for governmental subsidy in such cases, but also in the conversion process in general. This support, however, is a controversial issue, as it would mean increasing State interference in economic life; this is not universally favoured in market economy countries. Public financial support also raises the question of the extent to which the State machinery has the relative independence to encourage transition measures which are resisted, by e.g. the military industry on which the government, in turn, is partly dependent. In other words, although the conversion from military to civilian production is economically feasible - more so in the case of individual communities than in certain industries - it is not so certain that it is politically feasibly or possible in cases involving particular economic interests.(20)

To sum up, we may say that specialists have generally agreed on the following conclusions regarding the economic consequences of disarmament and the arms race:
the economic problems of diarmament are of two main types: maintaining the level of aggregate demand, and meeting structural concerns that affect particular areas and industries;
such problems can be minimized in all types of economies by advance planning;
advance planning requires detailed analysis of inter-industry estimates and unmet social needs (both domestic human concerns and aid to underdeveloped countries);
there is overwhelming agreement that disarmament would not cause economic depression, but would result eventually in productivity and growth for all economies.
These generalizations apply to studies on both national societies and specific industries. It is apparent, however, that industrial and occupational considerations lead to various other problems, including the reliance of present-day military spending on technology-intensive and research-intensive sectors such as electronics and aerospace industries. In these industries special measures are needed to offset negative repercussions, especially on the employment of engineers and workers. Problems are accentuated by the fact that these industries usually pay better wages and salaries than others, and are in most countries geographically concentrated.(21)

All these points indicate a strong need for a simultaneous consideration of the effects of arms races and disarmament measures. The arms race is a dynamic phenomenon, continuously shaping economic and social structures. Changes are seldom abrupt - rather, the effects of military spending are felt incrementally. The dynamic character of military spending, however, makes it quite difficult to achieve any "permanent" generally valid results in the analysis of the consequences of disarmament. To illustrate this point one need simply observe that these effects, and hence various conversion strategies, would have been quite different before weapons of mass destruction were invented or before weaponry had moved to capital-intensive and technology-intensive stages. Similarly, there are differences between cases or periods: relatively unorganized military establishments, and those institutionalized and closely connected with other important social forces.

Furthermore, there are significant differences between the phases in which military spending was a predominantly domestic phenomenon and those in which the activities of the military establishment and military industries have become transnationalized. These broad examples indicate, firstly, that a dynamic view of the economic and social consequences of the arms race and disarmament is needed and, secondly, that these two different, but related aspects of militarization must be explored in close connection to each other. Thirdly, the approach to the economic and social consequences of the arms race and disarmament should be sufficiently comprehensive. This means that research should not focus excessively on micro-level phenomena and quantitative studies, but that sufficient attention should also be given to broader analyses aiming at outlining alternative future structures of the international society in which disarmament is considered a central variable.(22) This type of research has so far not been common; more emphasis has been placed on the strategic, political and legal factors affecting the future of disarmament and arms control. A necessary perspective also involves linking the future military order of the world (by implication one of disarmament) with the New International Economic Order (NIEO). It is no exaggeration to say that the present military order of the world is a considerable obstacle to the realization of NIEO.(23) In the same vein we would say that disarmament would contribute, in some cases, perhaps only marginally, to carrying out, e.g. Unesco's tasks in the NIEO context. These tasks are, according to the Director-General of Unesco, autonomy in science and technology, the promotion of cultural identity and the fight against poverty.(24)

A full-scale analysis of the consequences of disarmament presupposes having sufficient information on the impact of military spending and military structures in general. This information could provide a baseline against which to compare the changes brought about by disarmament measures. In fact, many national case studies and international comparisons have been made of the military impact on industrial production, national information networks and education, political and administrative decision-making, and general attitudes in the countries concerned. However, there is a lack of comprehensive, systematic and reliable sources of information on which rational research projects and action programmes could be based.

3. THE IMPACT OF ARMS TRANSFERS ON MILITARIZATION AND DEVELOPMENT

Most studies that concentrate on the local consequences of disarmament on civil-military relations and military-industrial complexes tend to concentrate on the industrial countries. Many investigations on the local impact of the arms race treat the international environment as given and do not dwell, for example, on external military transactions. In fact, the only external aspect usually considered is the possible conversion of military spending into foreign aid. As repeatedly pointed out above, a much more comprehensive perspective is needed if account is to be taken - in particular in developing countries - of the real consequences of arms races, arms transfers and eventually of disarmament. A part of this perspective can be provided by the historical analysis of these phenomena.

3.1 Historical background

The history, in modern times, of what has come to be called the Third World is marked by military power, colonial wars and the use of violence for the sake of establishing domination and bringing about what is known today as the world market. This basic pattern, far from disappearing, is developing new dimensions and global ramifications. The scenarios of conflicts within societies in the periphery and between Third World nations are distinguished today by technological quantum jumps in destructive and repressive capacities provoked by an almost indiscriminate flow of arms and military software to the Third World. While ample evidence suggests an overall intensification of the conflict pattern in the periphery, the East-West confrontation is looming into the scenarios more than ever. The concern over a "deputy war" in the periphery converting into a global strategic confrontation is not far fetched. The relative ease with which tactical nuclear weapons - as opposed to the use of gas - have been assimilated into the prevailing military doctrines contribute to the likelihood of nuclear war fighting in a confrontation taking place in the Third World rather than, for instance, in Europe.

Equally important with concern about armaments, the role of the military, and the organization of violence and its relation to the Third World, however, is the amply documented and undenible fact that, for a growing proportion of the world population, misery is on the increase. Furthermore, the hope of overcoming this trend is dwindling as the Second Development Decade proclaimed by the United Nations seems to be degenerating into a decade of rearmament. The drain on resources imposed by military expenditure is but one aspect, though a serious one. Industrialization schemes, infrastructures and general development patterns needed to operate, service and assemble advanced weapon systems in several countries in the periphery might have even longer-lasting detrimental effects on development processes intended to fulfil the needs of peoples. The growing diversification and sophistication of means and tools needed to maintain and even reinforce the existing pattern of dominance through violence in its various forms receives little notice - mainly because obvious military hardware has a lesser share in the acquisition of armaments than such items as communication and electronic equipment and military software in general.

Any statistical enumeration of countries in which the military dominate the government would be outdated before the text gets into print. Untenable socio-economic conditions and contradictions appear throughout the Third World, and whatever the solution adopted, the military play a key role. This is why the continuing and often heated discussions about the causes of underdevelopment, and the sometimes mutually exclusive schemes for development need very urgently to be supplemented by an improved understanding of the role that armaments and the military take in shaping the present world order.

This bibliography offers a short but, it is hoped, representative introduction to the literature published since 1965, the year arbitrarily chosen because of the limitations imposed by space. Although earlier contributions are reflected in more recent publications, it may nevertheless be helpful to note briefly how the role of the military in developing areas was perceived in the literature over time, and where the limitations in the existing information and sources - diverse in scope and character - are located.

The building up of colonial empires can be analysed fairly accurately from existing archives, documents, autobiographical testimonies, novels and so on. Certain aspects of colonial history are brilliantly covered by historians, but much remains to be done. Not surprisingly, reports on the widespread resistance against colonial penetration are few and unreliable. The history of anti-colonial warfare and other forms of resistance may never be written, since most of those who left the records fought on the other side. The situation has never really changed in this respect, not even today, despite world-wide electronic news coverage. South Africa provides a good example. The day-to-day resistance against apartheid usually converts into what is euphemistically called "hard facts" in our press, and thence into scholarly writing, whenever circumstances force the white minority regime to release some figures - no matter how faulty - about people killed or wounded in resistance. It is easy to demonstrate that similar limitations to fact-finding on conflict manifestations in other parts of the periphery are the rule rather than the exception.

Not until the beginning of the twentieth century did the imperialist powers succeed in destroying most forms of militant resistance based on pre-industrial concepts of military organization. Only then did the army as a bureaucratic and centralized organization dependent on industrial inputs at an ever-increasing level become the universal form of military organization. The close association of late-comer industrialization and the ascendancy of militarism in Germany and Japan is but one indication of their mutually reinforcing character. The army materialized nationhood; its very existence provided the harsh social control necessary for rapid industrial accumulation and served as an important outlet for production in advanced sectors where neither German nor Japanese industry was competitive at the time. But it is also generally accepted that this particular breed of militarism led to the two World Wars. While the foundations of militarism have ever since remained a compelling subject for the social sciences, it is only since follow-up development has become the internationally accepted goal that Japan in particular has been looked upon as a possible model for successful late-comer industrialization.

3.2 Recent trends in social science

During the past two decades there has been a rapid increase in publications dealing with the role of the military in Third World countries, the majority, concerned with the role of the officer corps. Many social scientists were interested in analysing the capabilities of the military as agents of economic and social change. On the other hand, a whole body of literature on development research, international relations (especially international transfer relations), and theories about industrialization tends to ignore the role of arms and the military in the process of developing from underdevelopment. Even authors who analyse the colonial and neo-colonial dependence of the Third World, stressing the exploitative practices of industrialized countries, are remarkably reserved in examining the military and armaments.

Moreover, studies on the role of military factors and armaments from the standpoint of the Third World seldom analyse the totality of the prevailing situation. They have concentrated rather on the impact of these elements in the developing countries. This means that international transfers of arms, for example, have often been analysed in terms of demand factors, without paying due attention to those tendencies in the arms economies of the major supplier nations which push arms transfers to higher levels. One can go so far as to say that at present these supply factors, including the role of arms manufacturing transnational corporations, tend to determine the quantity and direction of arms more strongly than demand factors operating in recipient countries and regions. Furthermore, economic factors seem to have gained importance at the expense of political and military determinants.

As can be seen from this bibliography, most publications on arms transfers and military regimes in developing countries were not published in the countries concerned but in the West. This is due to the Western social science tradition of studying in depth the political processes of developing countries. In the 1950s and the early 1960s particularly, so-called area studies flourished and led to a great number of investigations in which the role of the military in various developing countries was highlighted and detailed. Many of them combined an analysis of the military establishment with the modernization theory which was the dominant paradigm in development research at the time. A natural outcome of this "alliance" was that the military element was seen as a main agent of modernization (defined as economic growth in the framework of the Western-dominated international division of labour) in several developing countries.

In many developing countries, the possibilities for studying arms imports, the production of weapons, or military activities in general are limited, except for publications in professional military journals. In particular if the military are in power, investigations on military activities by independent institutions are virtually impossible. In this situation, international organizations or regional research bodies could perhaps improve research by providing facilities and other support. In fact, FLACSO (Facultad Latinoamericana de Ciencias Sociales) in Latin America has started to do so by sponsoring a study on disarmament in Latin America. In a way this is natural, as certain Latin American countries have attempted during the last few years to curb conventional arms races in the region. In addition, the Tlateloko Agreement aims at keeping Latin America outside the nuclear arms race.

Other Latin American studies, in many cases influenced by the dependencia theory, have also been carried out on problems of military regimes and arms transfers. The most prominent exception to the general rule of non-existing research is India, where detailed studies have been undertaken not only of the Indian armed forces but also on problems of global disarmament, nuclear proliferation and strategic questions. By and large, studies from Africa, are also lacking.

Three main types of interpretation of the role of armaments and the military in the Third World (besides reference books) can be distinguished for the purpose of classification.

3.2.1 Publications stressing the effects of armaments and the military on development

Only in the 1960s did development sociologists and political scientists begin in a reasonably systematic way to study the role of the military in the periphery. The formulation of a theory of modernization resulted in a concentration of research mainly on élites as agents of social and economic change. The role of the military as a key group became the object of intensive research only after coups d'état in several African, Asian and Latin American countries. After the military had taken over political power more or less permanently in a number of countries in the Third World it was argued that the organizational capacity of the military, their

technological and managerial know-how and skills and social recruitment and cohesion made of this "rational" and organized institution a modernizing force in a traditional society.

The enormous transfers of weapons systems and know-how in arms technology, and attempts by several Third World countries to produce arms indigenously are hardly taken into consideration in economic development theory. If these factors are not ignored completely they are usually considered an external variable and therefore not included in the economic model. A few economists have examined defence expenditure as part of public expenditure and concluded that higher defence expenditure could have positive effects on the capacity for socio-economic development of Third World countries. After confronting so-called positive and negative effects of defence expenditure, the statistical results shows a high correlation of increased military expenditure and economic growth. While the statistical relation between high defence expenditure and high growth rates exists for a great number of Third World countries, this result can certainly not be interpreted, as is done occasionally, as a proof supporting the hypothesis that economic growth is a function of high defence expenditure. On the contrary, one must examine whether the causal relationship might be reversed: Does high economic growth in the industrial sector in Third World countries depend on social control and a polarization of the social system, requiring the expansion of the armed forces, and increased military expenditure and arms imports? So far, sociological and economic development theories have not been able to give conclusive answers to such problems. On the contrary, many important questions have not even been raised.

3.2.2 The arms transfer process

The drastically increased arms transfer process from industrialized to developing countries, the continuously increasing share of the Third World in world military expenditure, and the proliferation of modern weapons technology, including nuclear technology, has (especially during the 1970s) resulted in a growing number of publications. The transfers of major weapon systems are relatively well documented, including details on the type of weapons transferred, the value of the transfers, the supplier and the recipient countries. The most comprehensive description of the United States military aid programme, with information on United States military strategy and arms transfers to the Third World, appears in the annual hearings held by various committees of the United States Congress. (These documents are not included in the bibliography; for a complete list, consult the Monthly Catalog of United States Government Publications.)

Information on the transfer of small arms

and their use for internal repression is scanty. While the literature has no accepted theory regarding the determining factors for the supply of weapons, a variety of hypotheses are formulated and tested. The social and economic consequences of arms transfers are examined in only very few studies.

The use of weapons in the general militarization process observed in many countries, the absorption of scarce resources in the Third World, and the long-term effects on industrialization patterns of importing military-related technology, still remain to be examined. The general dynamics of armaments and the unsuccessful attempts at disarmament are criticized by the publications (with the explicit purpose of urging governments to spend a maximum of their resources on development instead of wasting limited funds on the military and armaments). Such studies (e.g. by the United Nations) point out that military expenditure is a hindrance to development. Most studies implicitly accept the premise that the level of military spending and the trend of "modernizing" of armed forces in the Third World can be altered and reversed without changing the country's existing social system and its integration into the world economy.

3.2.3 Professional publications on strategy and conflict theatres

While many books have been written on military strategy and tactics, the most up-to-date information on military planning, as far as Third World conflicts are concerned, can be obtained from military periodicals and special reports with limited circulation, e.g. RAND publications, usually prepared for defence institutions. While most of these publications are concerned mainly with developments in the military sector of industrialized countries, the Third World is not excluded. Military periodicals are valuable sources of information, expressing mainly official opinions and/or the interest of the armed forces and defence industry. Occasionally a self-assessment of the strategic situation, military strength, military production etc., is published by defence institutes in the Third World. Since no articles out of military journals and only some special reports are included in the bibliography, a list of the more important military periodicals, and also of journals independent of the military establishment, are listed in the Appendix.

4. RESEARCH TRENDS IN SOCIALIST COUNTRIES

It is worth noting that papers of scholars from countries with different social systems substantiate the conclusion that the arms race poses a serious threat to present and future generations. In this connection one should note how convincing the counter-criticism of the apologists of the arms race is. The latter speak of the "beneficial effect" of militarist preparations for international security, and of the technical impossibility of disarmament.

Scientifically substantiated facts about the negative consequences of the arms race in different spheres of economic and social life clearly point to the vital necessity of taking all possible opportunities to curb material preparations for war and to seek disarmament.

The possibility and beneficial consequences for all countries of such a change-over are recognized by many economists, sociologists and other scholars, including those represented in the bibliography. It is natural that these problems should be tackled differently in the socialist, Western and developing countries. However, investigations have demonstrated that, in all cases, conversion does not lead to insurmountable difficulties, and that the advantages it promises dwarf all transient difficulties which may arise.

A number of works deal with the economic and social implications of conversion in the postwar period. Soviet scholars, as well as authors from other countries, cite data to show that, in the context of a socialist economy, this process leads to a rapid growth of production for peaceful purposes and promotes the working people's standard of living. They are convinced that even a rapid implementation of radical disarmament measures, such as the reduction of armed forces, the cutting of defence spending, and so on, will not cause any economic or social difficulties if carried out in a well-arranged and systematic manner. At the same time the production, labour, scientific and other resources thereby released will make it possible to speed up the rates of economic development and raise public well-being in a short time. Scholars from the socialist countries also emphasize the economic and social benefits which disarmament will offer to other countries and to mankind as a whole. This, however, involves overcoming of the opposition of the social forces opposed to disarmament (e.g. monopolistic groups who benefit from the production and sale of arms).

The reorientation of material and labour resources is the subject of many papers contributed by Western authors. These, naturally, pay great attention to analysing the barriers and difficulties raised by socio-economic factors such as military-industrial complexes, the economic power of military concerns interested in the manufacture of arms, ways of overcoming unemployment among various categories of personnel as a result of disarmament, and so on.

Despite different social systems, common to all scholars whose works are referred to in this collection, is the desire to work out an economic programme for disarmament. They deal with a wide range of questions pertaining to the socio-economic consequences of disarmament (methods and forms of reconversion; the utilization of released resources for specific peaceful projects and programmes; the expansion of assistance to the developing countries, the role of international co-operation as a means of achieving a smoother transition to a disarmed world; consequences of disarmament for various social and professional groups, etc.). Their unanimous conclusion is that disarmament will promote a better economic and social situation throughout the world and create favourable conditions for the development of the world economy, education, science and culture.

Special mention should be made of searches for specific ways of utilizing resources which may be released as a result of disarmament, for solving the most acute socio-economic problems facing mankind, problems that call for intergovernmental and international co-operation: environmental protection, raw materials, foodstuffs, health, urbanization, employment, the development of culture and education and so on. The scientific analysis of these problems and well-grounded conclusions and recommendations will certainly help to rally public opinion for disarmament.

Notes and references

1. See Adamovic, Mihailo, "Economic aspects of disarmament". Proceedings of the International Peace Research Association Inaugural Conference. Assen 1966, p. 239-246.

2. See, e.g. Väyrynen, Raimo, "Militarization, conflict behavior and interaction: three ways of analysing the cold war". Tampere Peace Research Institute. Research Reports 3, 1973, p. 23-49.

3. Slater, Jerome & Nardin, Terry, The concept of a military-industrial complex, in Rosen, Steven (ed.), Testing the Theory of the Military-Industrial Complex. Lexington, Mass. 1973, p. 27-60.

4. Jahn, Egbert, "The role of the armaments complex in Soviet society (Is there a Soviet military-industrial complex?)". Journal of Peace Research, 3, 1975, p. 179-194.

5. For one exception see Russett, Bruce M., "The revolt of the masses: public opinion on military expenditures", in Russett, Bruce M. (ed.), Peace, War and Numbers. Beverly Hills, 1972, p. 299-320.
    This article does not go, however, deeper into the influences of the MICs on public opinion and intellectual climate.

6. See Albrecht, Ulrich, Transnationale Rüstungskonzerne in Westeuropa. Leviathan 1, 1974, p. 81-107, and Hagelin, Björn, Militär-industriellt samarbete i Västeuropa (Military-Industrial Cooperation in Western Europe). Stockholm 1977.

7. Galloway, Jonathan, "Multinational corporations and military-industrial linkages". International Studies Quarterly 4, 1972, p. 491-514.

8. See the studies annotated in Section II.

9. See, e.g. Albrecht, Ulrich; Ernst; Dieter; Lock; Peter; and Wulf, Herbert, Rüstung und Unterentwicklung. Iran, Indien, Griechenland/

Türkei: Die verschärfte Militarisierung. Reinbek bei Hamburg, 1976, p. 10-36.

10. See Sivard, Ruth Leger, World military and social expenditures, Leesburg, 1977.

11. See, for example, Russett, Bruce M., What price vigilance? Burdens of National Defense. New Haven, Yale University Press, 1972.

12. Dabelko, David and McCormick, James. Opportunity costs of defense: some cross-national evidence. Journal of Peace Research 2, 1977, p. 145-154 and Frederic Pryor, Public expenditures in communist and capitalist nations, London 1968, p. 120-126.

13. Albrecht, Ulrich, "Armaments and inflation". Instant Research on Peace and Violence 3, 1974, p. 157-167.

14. The situation seems to be somewhat similar even in middle-size countries like the United Kingdom, see Arthur Brown, "The effect of disarmament on the balance of payments of the United Kingdom", in Benoit, Emile (ed.), Disarmament and world economic interdependence. Oslo 1967, p. 115-137.

15. See, e.g., Huiskens, Ronald, The consumption of raw materials for military purposes. Ambio 5-6, 1975, p. 229-233.

16. See, e.g., Westing, Arthur, Ecological Consequences of the Second Indochina War. SIPRI, Almqvist and Wiksell. Stockholm 1976.

17. See references in Section II.

18. United Nations Secretary-General's Consultative Group, Economic and Social Consequences of Disarmament. New York 1962, p. 52.

19. See, e.g., Kurth, James, Aerospace production lines and American defense spendings, in Steven Rosen (ed.). Testing the Theory of the Military-Industrial Complex. D.C. Heath & Co., Lexington, Mass., 1974, p. 135-156.

20. In this connection it is interesting to observe the conclusion by Juliet Saltman that "economic feasibility as a focal concern has gradually come to be replaced by a deep and pervading recognition of political feasibility as the prime problem". In a more general context one may note another conclusion by Saltman that in the United States "a peak in disarmament and conversion studies was reached in 1965, diminishing after that time. This reduction reflected the growing involvement in the Viet Nam War", see Saltman, Juliet, Economic Consequences of Disarmament. Peace Research Reviews, Vol. IV, No. 5 (1972), p. 60 and 81.

21. This section relies heavily on Ibid. For a thorough British case study which largely confirms these generalizations, see The Economist Intelligence Unit, The Economic Effects of Disarmament. London 1963, 224 p. See also the comments by Stockholm Peace Research Institute on the United Nations Report, "Economic and Social Consequences of Military Expenditure", in Thee, Marek (ed.), Armaments and Disarmament in the Nuclear Age, A Handbook. Almqvist and Wiksell, Stockholm 1976, p. 200-203.

22. For one example of this sort of approach, see Falk, Richard, Arms control, foreign policy and global reform. Daedalus 3, 1975, p. 35-52.

23. Öberg, Jan, The New International Economic and Military Orders as Problems to Peace Research. Bulletin of Peace Proposals 2, 1977, p. 142-149.

24. See Unesco and the Establishment of a New World Order. Director-General's address to the 59th session of ECOSOC. Unesco Chronicle 9, 1975, p. 239-243.

Military periodicals and journals relevant to bibliography

a. <u>Official or semi-official military journals,</u> discussing strategic and military-industrial topics:

   - Allgemeine Schweizerische Militärzeitschrift (monthly, Switzerland)
   - Defense Management Journal (quarterly, U.S.A.)
   - Military Review (monthly, U.S.A.)
   - Défense Nationale (monthly, France)
   - Journal of the Royal United Services Institute (quarterly, United Kingdom)
   - Nato's Fifteen Nations (bi-monthly, Brussels)
   - Österreichische Militärzeitschrift (monthly, Austria)
   - Soviet Military Review (monthly, Soviet Union)
   - Militärwesen (monthly, GDR)
   - Wehrkunde (monthly, FRG).

b. <u>Arms technology journals,</u> discussing weapons development, technology and military-industrial topics:

   - Aerospace International (bi-monthly, FRG)
   - Armies and Weapons (bi-monthly, Switzerland)
   - Aviation Week and Space Technology (bi-weekly, U.S.A.)
   - Flight International (bi-weekly, U.S.A.)
   - Interavia (monthly, FRG)
   - Wehrtechnik (monthly, FRG).

c. <u>Branch information services,</u> giving detailed information for arms producers:

   - Defense Market Survey (monthly, U.S.A.)
   - International Defense Business (weekly, U.S.A.)
   - Milavnews (monthly, United Kingdom)
   - Wehrdienst (weekly, FRG).

d. <u>Publications of different armed forces in the U.S.A.:</u>

   - Air Force (monthly)
   - Armed Forces Journal International (monthly)
   - Marine Corps Gazette (monthly)
   - Navy International (monthly).

e. <u>Military and strategic journals published in developing countries or regions:</u>

   - Asian Defence Journal (quarterly, Malaysia)
   - Estrategia (bi-monthly, Argentina)
   - Institute of Defence Studies Analyses Journal (quarterly, India)
   - Pakistan Army Journal (monthly, Pakistan)

- Paratus (bi-monthly, Republic of South Africa)
- Revista Maritima Brasileira (quarterly, Brazil)
- United Services Institute Journal (bi-monthly, India).

f. Journals, independent of the military establishment:

- Adelphi Papers (IISS), (bi-weekly, United Kingdom)
- Antimilitarismusinformationen (monthly, FRG)
- Arms Control Today (monthly, U.S.A.)
- The Bulletin of Atomic Scientists (monthly, U.S.A)
- Campaign Against Arms Trade Newsletter (irregular, United Kindom)
- Defense Monitor (monthly, U.S.A.)
- North American Congress on Latin America Empire Report (monthly, U.S.A.)
- Survival (IISS) (monthly, United Kingdom).

g. Relevant peace research journals:

- Bulletin of Peace Proposals (Oslo, quarterly)
- Etudes Polémologiques (Paris, quarterly)
- Instant Research on Peace and Violence (Tampere, Finland, quarterly)
- Journal of Conflict Resolution (New Haven, Connecticut, U.S.A., quarterly)
- Journal of Peace Research (Oslo, quarterly)
- New Perspectives (Helsinki, quarterly)
- Peace and Change (Rohnert Park, California, U.S.A., quarterly)
- Peace Research in Japan (Tokyo, yearbook)
- Peace Research Reviews (Oakville, Canada, six issues in a volume)
- Pugwash Newsletter (London, four issues a year).

Reference books

Albrecht, G., Weyers Flottentaschenbuch, Munich (annual), English version published by the United States Naval Institute.

Archer, D. H. R., Jane's infantry weapons, London (annual).

Labayle-Couhat, J., Flottes de combat, Paris (bi-annual).

Moore, J., Jane's fighting ships, London (annual).

Moulton, J. L., Brassey's annual: defense and the armed forces, London (annual).

Owen, J. I. H., Brassey's infantry weapons of the world (annual).

Pretty, R. T., Jane's weapon systems, London (annual).

Senger and Etterlin, Taschenbuch der Panzer, Munich, several revised ed.

Stockhom International Peace Research Institute (SIPRI), Yearbook of world armaments and disarmament, Stockholm (annual).

Taylor, J. W. R., Jane's all the world's aircraft (annual).

The Chanakya defence annual, Allahabad, India (annual).

The International Institute for Strategic Studies (IISS), The military balance, London (annual).

Wiener, F., Die Armeen der NATO-Staaten, Vienna, several revised editions.

(Research guides are included in the bibliography.)

I. THE MILITARY ESTABLISHMENT, MILITARY INDUSTRY AND SOCIETY

This chapter focuses on studies which seek to illustrate the way in which the military establishment and military industry influence the structure of society as well as societal processes. Two trends can be discerned in this type of literature: one concentrating on civilian-military relations in political and social contexts, the other on what is usually known as the military-industrial complex, which is often analysed mainly in economic terms. A few studies explore the social and political consequences of disarmament, particularly in institutional terms.

1. Abrahamsson, Bengt, Military Professionalization and political power, with a foreword by Morris Janowitz. Beverly Hills, Sage Publications, 1972, 184 p.

    The study centres on the sociology of the military profession and observes its transformation as a function of social attitudes and other factors, identifying some key variables. The author examines the political power position of the military, surveys the problems of control, and examines the relationship between the military establishment and civilian society.

2. Fels, Reding, The economics of the military-industrial complex; papers presented at the 84th annual meeting of the American Economic Association. American Economic Review, vol. 62, May 1972, p. 297-318.

    In these papers, economic factors characterizing the American military industry and procurement are considered. Reich (in his "Does the United States economy require military spending?") argues that United States defence spending springs from the basic nature of a capitalist economy; military spending around 1950 was considered as the most convenient mechanism for the needed stimulation of the economy because social service expenditures are incompatible with a capitalist society. Melman, in his article "Ten propositions on the war economy", sees the United States war economy as differentiated from productive industry on both the micro- and macro-economic levels. Walter Adams makes a market-structure analysis of the military-industrial complex (MIC) and R. K. Kaufmann examines the position of aerospace firms in the governmental decision-making process.

3. Barnet, Richard J., The economy of death. New York, Atheneum, 1969, 201 p.

    Barnet examines the basic assumptions behind the defence budget to see what the taxpayer is getting for his money. The author explores the United States defence strategy and specifies rather exhaustively the costs of different defence sectors: he documents, for example, the waste in defence contracts. He considers the role of the military-industrial complex in setting national priorities and describes a programme of national conversion and the possibilities that citizens have for implementing such conversion.

4. Bletz, Donald F., The role of the military professional in United States foreign policy. Praeger special studies in United States economic and social development. New York, Praeger, 1972, 320 p.

    The study examines the changing role of the military professional in the formulation of foreign policy throughout the history of the United States, reviews the effect of the political role on the military profession, and makes recommendations for the profession in the future. The author presents arguments for and against the military's role in foreign policy decision-making.

5. Clark, John J., The economics of national defense, New York, Random House, 1966, 242 p.

    Clark applies micro-economic theory to weapon-systems analysis and to the description of conflicts between nation-States. The role of game theories in identifying risks and in finding out preferred solutions is examined. Moreover, Clark applies micro-theory to an analysis of power relationships between States and to the problems of economic warfare viewed as actions designed to enhance economic strength. Finally, the author examines the effects of war on economic progress.

6. Clayton, James L., The economic impact of the Cold War: sources and readings. New York, Harcourt Brac, 1970. 287 p.

The first articles emphasize the national and regional scope of defence expenditure and relate this expenditure to the civilian economy. Subsequent selections try to show how the Cold War generated economic pressures sufficient to change the nature of the market system itself. The impact of the war on science and the university is also considered; and economic consequences of the Viet Nam War are examined in six articles which also provide a summary chapter on the military-industrial-scientific complex.

7. Duscha, Julius, Arms, money and politics. New York, Van Rees Press, 1964, 211 p.

The author explores the economic and political problems that have become an integral part of defence programming. The book is an attempt to take a realistic look at the politics and economics of defence spending and to propose solutions for some of the problems it is raising. Duscha analyses the growth of United States miliary expenditure since the Second World War. The military-industrial complex - its rise, formation and growth - is discussed in detail. Many proposals concerning disarmament and its economic aspects are put forward.

8. Engelhardt, Klaus, et al., Militär-Industrie-Komplex im staatsmonopolistischen Herrschafts-system (The military-industrial complex under State monopolism). Berlin, Institut für Internationale Politik und Wirtschaft, 1974.

This work presents an analysis of the structure and politico-strategic and economic interest spheres of the MIC, of the role of profit interests, of the monopoly of the FRG in this sector, and of the approaches to armament research. These questions are examined in relation to the national-monopolistic system of government. A supplement contains a list of the persons belonging to the Military-Economic Working Group of the Ministry of Defence of the FRG (as of early 1972).

9. Enthoven, Alain, and Wayne, K. Smith, How much is enough? Shaping the defense program, 1961-1969. New York, Harper and Row, 1971, 346 p.

The book is largely concerned with the process of planning military strategy, forces and budgets in the Department of Defense, with particular emphasis on the role of the Systems Analysis Office in the planning process. The authors describe the principal management tools of the Secretary of Defense in developing and analysing military strategy and force requirements in 1961-1969.

10. Erickson, Wolfe, J.N., Erickson, John, The armed services and society: alienation, management and integration. Sixth Edinburgh seminar in the social sciences, 1969. Edinburgh, Edinburgh University Press, 1970, 170 p.

The papers deal with various aspects of the relationship between the armed forces and society. Topics include the society the armed forces serve; the efficiency of the military forces in relation to national security; whether and to what extent military training programmes adjust soldiers to reintegration into civilian society; and whether the services support or weaken the efforts of society at large. The main problem is to ensure that the armed services really remain the servants of society.

11. Fleckenstein, Bernhard, Bundeswehr und Industriegesellschaft (The armed forces and industrial society in the FRG). Boppard am Rhein, H. Boldt, 1971, 290 p.

Military officers, sociologists and lawyers analyse the problems associated with the presence of modern military forces in West German society. The underlying principles of the Bundeswehr and its position in society, its relations to institutions and the internal realm of the Bundeswehr are the main themes of the publication.

12. Försvarets Forskningsanstalt (FOA), Försvarsindustriella problem (Problems of defense industry). Stockholm 1975, 133 p.

The report explores in detail the economic impact of weapons production in Sweden and provides data on the interrelationships between military production and other sectors of the economy. Regional employment effects, technological and other costs of weapons procurement as well as trade in defence material are analysed. This report is a highly illustrative case study.

13. Galbraith, John Kenneth, How to control the military. New York, Doubleday and Company, 1969, 69 p.

This pamphlet explores the military-industrial complex: how it developed, how it wields power, how it can be controlled. The author explains why and how its power foundations are beginning to crumble. He offers both analysis and practical suggestions as to what can be done to control the military establishment.

14. Gleditsch, Nils Petter; Lodgaard, Sverre, Krigsstaten Norge (Norway: a warfare State). Oslo, Pax forlag, 1970, 155 p.

The authors present a case study of the impact of the military establishment on a society. They explore factors maintaining and controlling the warfare State and try to estimate its cost to Norway. There is a detailed analysis of the impact of the military on the research activities and on the topographic system of the country.

15. Government of India, Ministry of Defence, Report 1974-1975, New Delhi, 1975, 204 p.

Official annual report on India's national security, defence planning, the state of her armed forces, inter-service organizations and the activity of para-military forces. Details on defence production, research and development as well as diagrams of the administrative structure of several military organizations are included.

16. Harle, Vilho; Joenniemi, Pertti, Asevarustelun "valkoinen kirja": Tilastoja ja tietoja Suomen puolustuspolitiikasta (A "white book" on armament: facts and figures about Finnish defence policy). Tampere Peace Research Institute, Occasional Papers 5, 1976, 269 p.

This report is the only comprehensive attempt so far to map out the extent and development of the military establishment in Finland. It pays attention to military production, military spending, military research, arms trade and the general impact of the military effort on the Finnish economy. The report shows that even in a country with a relatively modest defence effort, the economic and social consequences are considerable.

17. Hickman, Martin B., (ed.), The military and American society. Beverly Hills, Glencoe Press, 1971, p. 167.

Essays on the nature and extent of the military domination of American life. Shoup and Fleming maintain that the role of the military has become too conspicuous; Leavitt and Hartly reject this thesis. McClelland advocates expanding the role of the military in the management of international conflicts. In a concluding statement, Galbraith suggests a "realistic programme for bringing the military into a responsible relationship" with the President and the Congress.

18. Holloway, David, Technology and political decision in Soviet armaments policy, Journal of Peace Research, vol. 11, no. 4 (1974), p. 257-279.

This article seeks to examine the processes of technological innovation in Soviet arms policy in the context of the current discussion about arms race dynamics: how are arms policies to be explained? It is commonly asserted both in the Soviet Union and outside that technological change is subordinated in the Soviet Union to close political control. The paper examines this proposition by looking at the institutional framework of the armaments complex and at the processes of innovation themselves. It emerges that innovation in military technology has been relatively successful because of the high priority given to it by the political leadership in terms of organizational arrangements, resources and attention. In spite of recent efforts to create roles and institutions with an interest in innovation, this is still the case. In this sense, innovation does depend upon political decision. The paper suggests, however, that this position is unsatisfactory, inasmuch as it ignores both the forces which guide the formation of political decision and the structural basis of the existing priorities.

19. Kovalenko, Ivan; Varis, Tapio, Public movements, mass media and disarmament. International détente and disarmament. Contributions by Finnish and Soviet scholars. Helsinki, Tampere Peace Research Institute, 1977, p. 241-260.

Kovalenko focuses on the role of public, nongovernmental organizations, national and transnational, in the activities promoting disarmament, peace and security. Varis, in turn, analyses the attitude of mass media to disarmament questions. He also outlines recent international trends in the grouping of various social forces in communication in relation to disarmament and arms race policies.

20. König, René, Beiträge zur Militärsoziologie (Contributions to military sociology). Cologne (Köln) 1969, 360 p.

These essays discuss the complex relationship between the military and civilian sectors of society, internal problems of the military leadership, its structure and motivations. Social stratification in the military leadership selection process and the effects of armament on the economy are studied.

21. Larson, Arthur D. (ed.), Civil military relations and militarism: a classified bibliography covering the United States and other nations of the world, with introductory notes. Kansas State University Library, 1971, 113 p.

A collection of materials dealing with civil-military relations and related fields. The bibliography concentrates on the United States, and other nations are included only by way of comparison.

22. Lens, Sidney, The military-industrial complex, London, Stanmore Press Ltd., 1971, 183 p.

Lens explores the origins and development of the military-industrial complex and its effects on United States society and foreign relations. The domestic effects of militarism are examined from the perspective of "internal imperialism". In the final chapter Lens puts forward a counter-programme to militarism and military waste.

23. Melman, Seymor, Pentagon capitalism: the political economy of war. New York, McGraw-Hill, 1970, 290 p.

The book starts from the analysis of State management, its structure and power "as a State within a State". Melman underscores the managerial primacy of the new control institutions within the Department of Defense. United States military expenditure is criticized, and investments in health services, education, housing, transport and foreign aid are compared with the military budget. A change in national priorities is considered necessary.

24. _____ . (ed.), The war economy of the United States. Readings on military industry and economy. New York, St. Martins Press, 1971, 247 p.

Melman brings together articles dealing with the

impact of military industry on the national economy; war economy and its implications for micro- and macro-economics. The authors (Barnet, Russett, Stone, Etzioni, Nossiter, etc.) analyse the growth and changes of the military economy in different sectors, the convertibility of military industry to civilian purposes, and the economic consequences of military industry for the economy as a whole. In the summary there is a "programme" for using the resources released for peaceful purposes; the impact on national production and employment, international economic relations, foreign aid and social consequences are considered.

25. Melman, Seymor, The permanent war economy, American capitalism in decline. New York, Simon and Schuster, 1974, 384 p.

The author surveys the workings of the military economy both at the firm and systemic levels and considers various unforeseen consequences of this economy, such as a decline in industrial efficiency and various social failures. Melman also pays detailed attention to conversion problems and prospects of the military economy, and concludes that the United States economy as a whole does not necessarily need military expenditure. He suggests, however, that abolishing the war economy requires that hierarchically organized State management of military production and military spending, be eliminated.

26. Morozov, G. et al., Public opinion in world politics. Social Sciences Today. Moscow, USSR Academy of Sciences, 1976.

Besides Morozov, contributors to this volume include V. Shaposhnikov, O. Kharhardin, A. Kalyadin, A. Berkov, A. Poltorak, E. Silin, E. Fyodorov and O. Baroyan. They analyse social processes and factors underlying the search for a more secure world peace, international co-operation and disarmament. The authors trace concrete manifestations of the influence of public opinion on problems of war and peace.

27. Moskos, Charles; Hills, Berky (ed.), Public opinion and the military establishment. Beverly Hills, Sage Publications, 1971, 294 p.

The articles deal with military education and civilian values, civilian response to military roles, the relationship between the armed forces and United States society. Essays also examine societal definitions of the military establishment and the impact of public attitudes.

28. Pursell, Carrol W. (ed.), The military-industrial complex. New York, Harper-Row, 1972, 342 p.

The authors analyse the origins and growth of the military-industrial complex and its effects on United States society. The critical question is whether different groups, including the MIC, tend to act in concert to reinforce each other, or whether they are countervailing forces, tending to keep each other in check. The analyses investigate the problem of the MIC in its historical context. Theoretical aspects of the complex are also examined.

29. Republic of South Africa, Department of Defence, White paper on defence and armament production, 1973, p. 22.

This document provides a detailed account of the military status of the apartheid regime and the strategy proposed in 1973, including the planning of the arms production sector.

30. Rosen, Steven (ed.), Testing the theory of the military-industrial complex. Lexington, Mass., D.C. Heath & Co., 1973, 311 p.

This reader contains both theoretical and empirical analyses of the MIC, mainly in the United States. Some contributions show the relatively close connection between United States military spending and the development of its military establishment on the one hand and some of the characteristics of the economy on the other. The main conclusion is, however, that the MIC does not determine military development to the extent sometimes claimed. This conclusion is elaborated in an article by Jerome Slater and Terry Nardin.

31. Russett, Bruce M., The revolt of the masses: public opinion on military expenditures, in Russett, Bruce M. (ed.), Peace, war and numbers. Beverly Hills, Sage Publications, 1972, p. 299-319.

Before the 1960s only a small minority of the United States population favoured reducing the armed forces. A somewhat larger minority rather consistently advocated expanding the military, but at most times a majority of the population either expressed satisfaction with the existing defence effort or was indifferent. By the late 1960s this situation had changed markedly, partly due to the Viet Nam War. In recent soundings a near-majority of the entire population has regularly advocated a reduction in military spending. Russett also shows that anti-militarism is now strongest among the informed public.

32. Senghaas, Dieter, Rüstung und Militarismus (Armaments and militarism). Frankfurt am Main, Suhrkamp Verlag, 1972, 370 p.

The author starts with an introductory analysis of the present problem of militarism and extends it to an investigation of the role of "threat politics" in international relations. The major part of the study is devoted to a detailed analysis of various aspects of the United States armaments complex and its development. While the book is fairly theoretical, it also contains practical descriptive and statistical information.

33. Sirjaques, Françoise, Determinanten der französischen Rüstungspolitik (Determinants of French armaments policy). Frankfurt/Main, Frankfurter Beiträge zur Friedens- und Konfliktforschung, 1976.

A comprehensive description of the French State bureaucracy and administrative procedures for armaments. The role of arms production in post-war economic policy in France is evaluated and the importance of arms exports is emphasized. The problem of accounting for arms is discussed in detail.

34. Weidenbaum, Murray, Peacetime defense. New York, Praeger Publishers. 1972, 194 p.

Weidenbaum's book is a general analysis of the United States defence economy and largely relies on the co-ordination and compilation of data published earlier. The author considers the costs of defence, relations between the military and industry, military profits and waste, the role of the military as an employer, as well as the geographical allocation of military contracts in the United States. Separate chapters are also devoted to the overseas operations of the military and its impact on scientific research in the country. Weidenbaum provides a readable general analysis of social and economic effects of military spending in the United States.

35. Yarmolinsky, Adam (special editor), The military and American society. The Annals of the American Academy of Political and Social Science, vol. 406, March 1973, 268 p.

This collection of articles pays attention to three broad areas: the functions of the military establishment from the standpoint of United States foreign policy; implications for the national economy, including technology and balance of payments; relations between the military establishment and other institutions in American society. The institutional analysis focuses on the professionalism of soldiers, race problems in the armed forces, the utilization of women in the military and on various questions of military research. All in all, the volume provides a fairly comprehensive analysis of the social role played by the United States military establishment.

II. ARMS RACE, DISARMAMENT AND THE ECONOMY

This chapter focuses on the purely economic aspects of the arms race and disarmament; studies dealing with the wider politico-economic and structural implications are excluded. There are three sections: military spending and economic development; general descriptive analyses of the economic consequences of disarmament; detailed quantitative investigations of such consequences, usually in regional or domestic settings.

II.1 Economic consequences of the arms race

36. Benoit, Emile, Defence and economic growth in developing countries. Lexington, Mass., Lexington Books, 1973, 326 p.

The effects of military expenditure and arms production on the economic growth of six developing countries between 1950 and 1965 are analysed. The main statistical finding is that average defence burdens (military spending as per cent of national product) correlated positively, not inversely, with the countries' growth rates. The main hypotheses were tested in an extensive case study on India and in national studies on Mexico ("Low defence burden benefits growth"), South Korea ("Development through defence"), Israel ("Growth in a siege economy"), the United Arab Republic ("Defence overshadows development"), and Argentina ("Defence in politics").

37. Boulding, Kenneth; Gleason, Alan, War as an investment: The strange case of Japan. Peace Research Society (International) Papers, vol. III (1965), p. 1-17.

The authors present a historical analysis of the costs and benefits of the military industry in Japan since the 1850s. The main conclusion is that in the early days of the period the military industry may have been spearheading modernization, but during the first half of the twentieth century costs became enormous, while returns remained small. After the war, the low degree of military spending facilitated the rapid economic growth of Japan.

38. Deutenmüller, Jörg, Die Entwicklung der Militärausgaben von der Reichsgründung bis zur Gegenwart und ihr Einfluss auf das Wirtschaftswachstum (The development of military expenditure from the founding of the FRG to the present day and their impact on economic growth). Reinheim 1971, 148 p.

The author examines the development of military expenditure in West Germany by functional categories, their influence on economic growth from 1951 to 1968 and their effects on the labour force, real capital formation, and technological progress. The study maintains that military spending has promoted the growth of the West German economy, although not in a uniform and quantifiable manner.

39. Dobosiewicz, Z., Ekonomicane skutki zbrojen w krajach rozwijajacych sie (Economic effects of armaments in the developing countries). Sprawy Miedzynarodowe. (Warszawa) no. 5, 1973, p. 38-47.

On the basis of an analysis of the economic situation in the developing countries, the author concludes that in most of these States, high expenditure for military purposes adversely influences their overall growth. The article outlines the structure of military spending in Third World countries and reasons for the recent rise in this expenditure. Finally, the author discusses the role played by the armed forces in the developing countries and prospects for reforms which could change the present situation.

40. Doernberg, Stefan, Die Abrüstungsfrage im Wechselverhältnis politischer, ökonomischer und

sozialer Aspekte (The problem of disarmament in the interplay of political, economic and social aspects). IPW-Berichte, Berlin 3, 1974, p. 2-11.

This analysis deals with armaments as a constant threat to peace, the relationship between political détente and disarmament and the complicated, but not insoluble, problems of conversion from armaments to peace production. The continuously growing burden people have to bear because of armaments and the possibilities of using resources released by disarmament in solving urgent socio-economic problems are studied. This study is substantiated by many facts and figures.

41. Dolgu, Gheorghe, Economy and armaments. Bucurest, Editura politicas, 1974.

An extensive study which deals with the profound implications of the present-day arms race for the economic situation of every country, and for the international economic situation. Special reference is made to military budgets, inflation and economic crises.

42. Dumas, Lloyd J., Thirty years of the arms race: The deterioration of economic strength and military security. Peace and Change, vol. 4, no. 2 (1977), p. 3-9.

The author aims at showing that far from being a source of economic strength and/or a guarantor of prosperity, sustained high levels of military spending have produced a serious cumulative deterioration in the foundation of the United States economy. In his view the United States has reached the point at which increases in the size of her military systems produce ever greater deterioration in the military aspect of national security. Hence a substantial reduction in the size of the military system, with concommitant major reductions in military expenditure, has become an absolutely critical element in a realistic strategy for effectively revitalizing the economy and increasing the national military security.

43. Gottheil, Fred M., An economic assessment of the military burden in the Middle East: 1960-1980. Journal of Conflict Resolution, vol. 18, no. 3, September 1974, p. 502-513.

The article shows that the military burden in the Middle East for 1960-1969 and 1970-1980 is not only substantial but escalating at an almost pathological rate. In the Middle East, a region of low per capita income and not especially endowed with an abundance of natural resources, the costs of military spending are particularly severe. A variant of the Harrod-Domar model is used in the measurement of these costs. Gottheil concludes that military spending has produced and will continue to produce a substantial misallocation of human and material resources, and that it is difficult to envisage real economic development in the Middle East under such conditions.

44. Klein, Peter, Thesen zur Abrüstungsfrage (Theses on the question of disarmament), IPW-Berichte, Berlin 1, 1972.

The socio-economic problems of disarmament are discussed. The necessity of disarmament is substantiated and the social forces in favour of arms limitation and disarmament, as well as the obstacles they are confronted with, are examined. The successes achieved so far in the form of bilateral and multilateral agreements between countries outside and within the United Nations and the prospects for disarmament are dealt with in detail.

45. Lock, Peter; Wulf, Herbert, Wachstum durch Rüstung? Zum Zusammenhang von wirtschaftlicher und militärischer Sicherheit (Growth by armaments? On the relationship between economic and military security) Blätter für deutsche und internationale Politik no. 4, 1977, p. 413-433.

Demands for disarmament and the prohibition of arms exports are frequently countered by groups with vested interests, who argue increasing employment problems and retardation of economic growth. With reference to the situation in the FRG, the authors conclude that, besides the negative effects for the development in the Third World, arms exports cannot be considered as a contributing factor to economic growth in the supplier countries. On the basis of the theory of export-included growth it is shown that, in countries with high military expenditure, the competitiveness of certain industrial sectors has been decreased, while in countries with low military expenditure or delayed rearmament (as in Japan and in FRG) industry has experienced high rates of exports, which in turn have led to high growth rates of GNP.

46. Regling, Horst, Militärausgaben und wirtschaliche Entwicklung, dargestellt unter besonderer Berückssichtigung der Verhältnisse in der Bundesrepublik Deutschland seit 1955 (Military expenditure and economic development with special reference to the conditions in the FRG since 1955). Hamburg, Verlag Weltarchiv, 1970, 265 p.

The study examines the influence of military spending on the defence economy as well as on other sectors of the economy using statistical data from the United States, the United Kingdom and the Federal Republic of Germany. The author evaluates the effects of military expenditure on the growth of economies in general and on that of the Federal Republic in particular. The conclusion is that disarmament efforts deserve priority, even if they may slow down economic growth.

47. Subrahmanyam, K., Indian defence expenditures in global perspective. Economic and Political Weekly, vol. VIII, June 1973, p. 1155-1158.

World military expenditure, declining to about 6 per cent of the GNP in the 1970s, is still well above the Indian rate. Countries around India - such as Pakistan, Iran and China - spend far above the world percentage. Contrary to popular belief, high defence expenditure in India does not seem to have a negative correlation with high economic growth.

48. Subrahmanyam, K., Our national security. New Delhi 1972, 65 p.

For a developing country like India, with the potential to develop into a major power, national security is more than merely defence. It also means industrialization. The two tasks of industrialization and building up military power will have to be undertaken simultaneously if India is to be respected as an independent decision-making centre. Despite social and economic problems, as long as the industrial proletariat, the middle-class and small farmers are kept tolerably satisfied with expectations of mobility into higher income groups, the system can be considered manageable. India will have to develop further her nuclear option and at the same time make efforts to gain self-sufficiency in the production of weapons.

49. Kruglyj Stol "Me i Mo" - Social ekonomiceskie aspekty gonki voorruzenij i razoruzenija (The round table of MEiMO - social-economic aspects of armaments competition and disarmament). Mirovaja ékonomika i mezdunarodnye otnosenija (Moskva), no. 2, 1976, p. 81-99.

The participants were prominent Soviet economists, sociologists, historians, researchers working in the institutions of the Academy of Sciences of the USSR (V. Aboltin, V. Yemelyanev, Y. Andreev, T. Belans, V. Borisov, V. Vaneev, N. Ivanov, A. Kalyadin, M. Pertnoi, B. Sakoznikov and I. Zulev). Contributors analyse the effects of the arms race on some aspects of contemporary society, as well as the consequences, problems, and tasks which could emerge as a result of implementing disarmament measures. Particular attention has been devoted to an analysis of concrete manifestations of the harmful impact of the modern arms race on the world economic situation, on the position of the developing nations, and on the standard of living of working people. Alternative uses of the economic, scientific and human resources employed in the military sector have been examined (for example, improvement of the environment, exploration of the ocean floor and of outer space, solution of world energy and food problems, expansion of East-West trade).

50. United Nations, Department of Economic and Social Affairs, Disarmament and development, Report of the group of experts on the economic and social consequences of disarmament. New York 1973, 37 p.

Prepared under the chairmanship of Swedish diplomat Alva Myrdal, the report draws attention to the interrelationships between disarmament measures and development. Concrete examples of how unfavourably development aid and health

expenditure compare to military spending and particularly to military research and development, are given. If disarmament can be achieved, the "dividend" will differ significantly among nations according to their present level of spending. High "disarmament dividends" should be converted into development aid.

51. United Nations, Department of Political and Security Council Affairs, Economic and social consequences of the arms race and of military expenditures, New York 1972, 51 p.

Prepared by a group of experts appointed by the Secretary-General of the United Nations in 1971, the report reviews in detail the manifold aspects of armament dynamics during the 1960s. Qualitative aspects of the arms race are analysed as well as its impact on resources. Military research and development are considered a key element in stimulating the arms race. Far-reaching negative consequences of military considerations are noted, such as distortion of international trade patterns and continuous impediments to development.

52. Zentralvorstand der Gewerkschaft wissenschaft für die Weltföderation der Wissenschaftler (ed.), ABC-Waffen, Abrüstung und Verantwortung der Wissenschaftler. Raport über eine internationale Konferenz der Weltföderation der Wissenschaftler, Berlin (DDR), 21-23 November 1971 (ABC weapons, disarmament and the responsibility of scientists. Report on an international conference of the World Federation of Scientific Workers, Berlin (GDR), 21-23 November 1971). Berlin n. d., 246 p.

Contributors include M. V. Ardenne (Disarmament and public welfare), B. Graefrath (Aspects of the disarmament problem relating to international law), W. Krutzsch (The attitude of the GDR to prohibiting biological and chemical weapons), J. Kuczynski (The social and economic consequences of disarmament), K. Lohs (Economic problems in the destruction of chemical weapons), G. Schumann (Technical control and non-proliferation of nuclear weapons) and P. A. Steiniger (The possibilities of the legal protection of scientists in the fight against weapons of mass destruction).

II.2 General analyses of the economic consequences of disarmament

53. Aboltin, V. Ja (ed.), Politika gosudarstv i razoruženie (Politics of States and disarmament). Three volumes, Moscow, Izdatel´stvo Nauka, 1967.

This three-volume publication contains an analysis of the post-war policies of the major States and of the main regions (Europe, Asia, America, Africa) regarding the various issues of arms limitation and disarmament. Social and economic effects of the arms race on individual countries and regions are considered in detail and alternative uses of military expenditure and war industries are suggested.

54. Aboltin, V. Ja (ed.), Sovremennye problemy razoruženija (Contemporary problems of disarmament). Moscow, Izdatel'stvo Mysl', 1970, 397 p.

The authors consider strategic, political and economic problems connected with the arms race and disarmament. The book includes chapters on specific partial measures connected with political and military détente, on military-political theories and concepts related to the arms race and arms control, on military assistance and the arms trade, on the social and economic consequences of the arms race and disarmament, and on problems of security arrangements under conditions of disarmament.

55. Benoit, Emile; Boulding, Kenneth, Disarmament and the economy. New York, Harper & Row 1963, p. 310.

This reader makes a systematic study of the impact of potential disarmament measures on various economic, financial and labour questions. It dwells not so much on detailed quantitative explorations as on descriptive and analytic consideration of the impact of disarmament and of adjustment measures, verification costs, impact on R&D, monetary aspects and balance-of-payment problems.

56. Bolton, Roger (ed.), Defense and disarmament. The economics of transition. Englewood Cliffs, Prentice-Hall, 1966, 180 p.

These essays by economists, industrial managers and policy planners deal with disarmament and the possibilities of its implementation from an economic perspective. They touch upon the transfer of defence-industry resources to civilian uses, labour-market problems, the impact of arms reductions on research and development and foreign aid. The reply by the United States Arms Control and Disarmament Agency to the United Nations Secretary-General on the economic and social consequences of disarmament is also included.

57. Von Bredow, Wilfried (ed.), Ökonomische und soziale Folgen der Abrüstung. Texte aus West- und Osteuropa. Cologne, Pahl-Rugenstein, 1974, 210 p. (English version: Economic and social aspects of disarmament. Contributions from East and West Europe. Varanasi (India), BPP Publications, 1974, 172 p.)

This reader consists of 13 papers, eight from the West and five from the East, originally presented at the Symposium on Economic and Social Aspects of Dsarmament in Berlin (GDR) in November 1973. The authors consider interrelationships between political and economic factors and disarmament. Armament dynamics and various types of interests associated with it are explored. Several articles are devoted to the analysis of conversion problems in the Soviet Union and in the West. The role of disarmament in relations between centrally-planned and market-economy countries is investigated.

58. Disarmament and Development, Development dialogue, vol. 5, no. 1 (1977), p. 3-33.

This special section of the publication by the Dag Hammarskjöld Foundation, Sweden, contains an introduction and articles by Alva Myrdal and Frank Barnaby. Myrdal analyses the East-West arms race, and Barnaby the background of armaments process in the Third World. Barnaby reviews the extent of world military spending, the arms trade, arms production in the Third World, and the production of nuclear weapons. The introduction analyses relationships between disarmament and development, international and national for both industrialized and developing countries.

59. Kaldor, Mary; Curnow, R.; McLean, M.; Robinson, J.; Shephard, P.; General and complete disarmament. A systems-analysis approach. Futures, vol. 8, no. 5 (1976), p. 384-396.

The authors propose a two-phased approach to the study of general and complete disarmament: a synthesis of past research to portray the social roles of armament, and an attempt to understand the policy implications of a reversal of armament trends. The development of dynamic models, through the application of structural modelling and the expansion of the historic data base, would allow the assessment of alternative paths to general and complete disarmament. The authors recognize the limitations of systems analysis, and stress the need to involve a wide audience in the evaluation of the results.

60. Kopal, V., OSN a základy mírového režimu morského dna (The United Nations and the foundations of a peaceful regime for the sea-bed). Casopis pro mezinárodníprávo (Czechoslovak Journal for international law), 1971, no. 3, p. 245-257.

As analysis of the documents adopted by the 25th session of the General Assembly of the United Nations, which laid the foundation for the contemporary peaceful arrangements governing the sea and ocean beds, and stipulated further measures to complete international legal arrangements.

61. Lada, I. V., Esli mir razoružit'sja (If the world is to be disarmed). Moscow, Izdatel'stvo Mezdunarodnye Otnošenija, 1961.

The book describes the potential use of resources now consumed by the arms race for various Soviet and foreign projects of a global character (e. g. changing the earth's climate, reclaiming deserts and permafrost areas, establishing intercontinental transport lines, installations to produce cheap electric power).

62. Lindberg, Niels, The conflict theory and economic depressions, with some views on various political aspects of an anti-depression programme as supplementary to armament cuts, in Proceedings of the International Peace Research Association

Second Conference, Vol. II, Poverty, development and peace. Assen, Van Gorcum, 1968, p. 111-123.

The author tries to visualize a policy to prevent depressions in the event of large military cuts, not only as a supplementary policy, but as an essential long-term peace strategy. He also discusses the consequent political difficulties and appears to conclude that such difficulties are more serious than the economic ones.

63. Meyers, William (ed.), Conversion from war to peace: social economic and political problems. New York 1972, 121 p.

The book is compiled from two conferences, held in 1969 and 1971. Military roadblocks to conversion, the role of industry and government, the impact of the conversion process on minorities, options available for using the conversion process are examined. The authors investigate the effects of reduced military spending on the social sector, health care, housing, environment, education, transport and so on.

64. Morozov, V. A., Razoruženie i problemy kapitalisti̇českogo rynka (Disarmament and the problems of the capitalist market), Moscow, Izdatel´stvo Mysl´, 1964.

The book deals with the following: marketing problems involved in the development of war industries; objective opportunities for disarmament and economic development for peaceful purposes; switchover from war industry to civilian non-military production; prospects of market expansion through the abolition of military loans and taxes.

65. Report from Iron Mountain on the possibility and desirability of peace, with introductory material by Leonard C. Lewin. London, MacDonald, 1968, 141 p.

This is a fictitious report allegedly prepared between 1963 and 1966 by an anonymous high-level special study group of 15 with academic and other distinctions, under the auspices of the United States Government. It deals with the implications of world peace for the long-term stability and performance of United States society. The effects of disarmament on the economy and on social welfare are discussed in the light of various "disarmament scenarios". This leads the group to dicuss non-military functions of war and the arms race, and their impact on the viable transition to a peaceful world. The chilling conclusion of the report is that the continuation of wars and arms races is a stabilizing factor for which it would be very difficult to find satisfactory substitutes. This book is discussed by Henry S. Rowen, Anatol Rapoport, Jessie Bernard, Marc Pilisuk, Kenneth Boulding, Murray Weidenbaum, Leonard Duhl and Bruce M. Russett in Kenneth Bouding (ed.), Peace and war industry. New York, Aldine Publishing Company, 1970, p. 53-82.

66. Saltman, Juliet, The economic consequences of disarmament. Peace Research Reviews, vol. 4, April 1972, 88 p.

This review presents a chronological analysis of studies dealing with the economic consequences of disarmament. The studies are grouped according to three criteria: regional, occupational, and industrial considerations. The general conclusion is that it is possible to disarm without major economic difficulties, provided that sufficient advance planning is undertaken.

67. Sivard, Ruth Leger, World military and social expenditures 1976. Leesburg, Virginia, WMSE Publications, 1976, 32 p.

Detailed statistics of an arms race costing close to US $300,000 million annually are confronted with indicators of the unmet needs of society, special attention being paid to the potential for destruction and the heavy burden on the world economy. Tables with data on 132 countries relate the expenditure and the absorption of resources for the military as compared to education, nutrition and health. A follow-up report to this publication was produced in 1977 by Sivard and published by WMSE Publications.

68. World Federation of Scientific Workers, The role of scientists and of their organizations in the struggle for disarmament. Scientific World 3-4, 1975, 68 p.

This special issue of Scientific World contains reports from a conference held in Moscow in July 1975. Most of the speeches and reports deal directly or indirectly with economic aspects of disarmament, including Professor J. M. Legay's "Social and economic aspects of disarmament: the economic burden of the arms race and the problems of scientific workers" (p. 19-24). Legay's report considers the distortion of economic and scientific development by the arms race, the use of raw materials in the arms race, the role of transnational corporations in the arms race, the prevention of unemployment in a disarming world, and the role of international economic co-operation in the transition to peace without weapons.

69. Emel´Janov, V. S., Atom i mir (Atom and peace). Moscow, Atomizdat, 1967.

The book discusses various aspects of the utilization of atomic energy. Emphasis is placed on the problems of disarmament, including those of verification, the nuclear test ban, and the nonproliferation of nuclear weapons.

II. 3 Specific analyses of the economic consequences of disarmament

70. Anderson, Forrest P., Defence cutbacks: Some effects and solutions. Washington, D. C.,

Industrial College of the Armed Forces, 1971, 38 p.

This study examines the background of local dependence of defence spending: the effects on two communities of cutbacks in defence expenditure, and ways in which adverse effects on the local economy can be avoided.

71. Chatterji, Manas, Local impact of disarmament, foreign aid programmes and development of poor-world regions: a critique of Leontief and other growth models. Peace Research Society (International) Papers, vol. IV (1966), p. 39-65.

Chatterji evaluates contributions by Leontief, Suits, Isard and Schooler. He suggests that they open up new directions in economic research on disarmament, but also contain imperfections, mainly technical. A comment by Théodore Ponzen (p. 67-75) refers to efforts to accumulate empirical knowledge on the subject.

72. Duisenberg, W. F., The economic consequences of disarmament in the Netherlands. Journal of Peace Research, vol. 2 no. 2, 1965, p. 177-186.

The impact of military spending on the Dutch economy is explored in some detail. The author suggests that the harmful effects of disarmament can generally be neutralized by special government measures, provided that individual firms prepare themselves for the discontinuation of defence orders. In such circumstances, disarmament may even stimulate economic growth.

73. Dyckman, John W., Some regional development issues in defence programme shifts. Journal of Peace Research, vol. 1, no. 3-4, 1964, p. 191-203.

The author shows how the pattern of United States defence expenditure has reinforced certain industrial and urban development shifts and, by accelerating the growth of certain urban areas, has created local situations of great volnerability. The shift to California has changed the structure and character of the industrial life of the State and has, for instance, made of the defence industry complex, California's principal export industry. Under conditions of rapid and sizeable reduction of military expenditure, California would face serious problems of reduced demand for its exports and for specific skills.

74. Isard, Walter; Schooler, Eugene, An economic analysis of local and regional impacts of reduction of military expenditure. Peace Research Society (International) Papers, vol. I, 1964, p. 15-44.

The writers try to compute the local and regional effects of a reduction of military spending in six areas of the United States. They conclude that, with proper conversion programmes, adverse effects of the cutback can be avoided in all regions investigated; and, in the long run, alternative investments can lead to increased economic welfare.

75. Joenniemi, Pertti; Kaaretsalo, Pentti, Suomi ja aseidenriisunta (Finland and disarmament). Helsinki, Tammi, 1970, 112 p.

The first half of this book deals with general problems of disarmament and its economic and social consequences. The latter part examines, with the aid of input-output analysis, the impact of potential disarmament measures on production, employment, foreign trade and research. The authors conclude that disarmament would not produce any great economic difficulties in Finland, with the partial exception of unemployment.

76. Leontief, Vassily, Disarmament, foreign aid and economic growth. Journal of Peace Research, vol. 1, no. 3-4, 1964, p. 155-167.

The paper is concerned with the possible effects of disarmament and capital transfers. These effects are examined for both the developed and underdeveloped areas of the world. An aggregative growth model is developed to study quantitatively the impact of alternative capital transfers, through foreign aid and disarmament policies, on growth rates in these areas. The projected effects of a possible sample of such policies over a ten-year period (1959-1969) are summarized. Leontief's paper is commented upon by Josef Sebestyen of the Hungarian Academy of Sciences.

77. Lynch, John E., Local economic development after military base closures. New York, Praeger Publishers, 1970, 350 p.

Twelve cases of base closures are studied. Impact naturally varied from one case to another. In general, in most cases, unemployment and other economic losses were avoided during the conversion. The study indicates that the threat of closing leads to joint action in the community to counteract the effects even before the closure takes place - usually in a wider context than the purely local one.

78. Mack-Forlist, Daniel; Newman, Arthur, The conversion of shipbuilding from military to civilian markets. New York, Praeger Publishers, 1970, 209 p.

The study indicates that the United States shipbuilding industry is in danger of complete collapse if military spending in this sector is abolished or drastically curtailed; it can be developed into a viable civilian industry only by extensive government aid, which is needed in any case. Total employment in 13 major yards amounted in 1967 to only 85,000: hence the question is not of major importance from the standpoint of the economy as a whole.

79. Report of the Committee on the Economic Impact of Defense and Disarmament, Washington, D.C., United States Government Printing Office, 1965, 92 p.

The report considers the general economic impact of the United States defence expenditure and its interrelations with national economic goals. Most of it is based on an analysis of various ways of adjusting to changes in military spending and the operability of the governmental machinery in facilitating such an adjustment. It suggests many measures for governmental policy and considers information and research needs. Although largely an administrative document, the report contains a lengthy statistical annex on the impact of military spending on the United States economy.

80. Russett, Bruce M., What price vigilance? The burdens of national defense. New Haven and London, Yale University Press, 1970, 261 p.

Russett explores defence spending, mostly quantitatively, by US States and senatorial roll-call behaviour, distribution of defence expenditure within military alliances in the light of the theory of collective goods, and the opportunity costs of defence in the United States, Canada, France and Britain during the twentieth century. He provides some theoretical explanations for the soaring military budgets, and a diagnosis and prognosis of the role of the military in United States society.

81. Udis, Bernhard (ed.), The economic consequences of reduced military spending. Lexington, Mass., D.C. Heath & Co., 1974, 398 p.

This reader deals with the impact of disarmament on aggregate economic activity, its regional and local impact, the adjustment of Department of Defense manpower, balance-of-payments impact of a Viet Nam disengagement, organization and administrative factors affecting shifts in defence spending. The conclusions suggest a relatively easy transition period. However, projected employment data reveals that some areas heavily dependent on military spending could face serious problems. Advance planning and co-operation by the parties involved is required to prevent this from happening otherwise the report concludes that the United States possesses sufficient vitality and flexibility to absorb the consequences of reduced military spending without serious dislocations.

82. United States Arms Control and Disarmament Agency, Economic impact of military base closings, vols. I & II. Washington, D.C., ACDA/E-90, 1970, 280 + 260 p.

This report analyses 80 military base closings, nine in detail, to study community impact and adjustment to closings. The communities adjusted economically and psychologically more easily than anticipated. Some had unemployment problems, but their severity was dependent not on the speed of closing but on the general state of the local economy.

83. _____ The economic impact of reductions in defense spending. Washington, D.C., 1972, 31 p.

The report summarizes the principal findings of most of the 29 research projects on the consequences of reduced defence spending that were sponsored by the Arms Control and Disarmament Agency. Effects of military cutbacks on the national economy, industries, regions, communities and individual workers are explored. Reductions in military spending seemed likely to produce transitional problems in the economy, but total output and employment would be sustained.

III. ARMS TRADE AND MILITARY ASSISTANCE: INTERNATIONAL AND NATIONAL IMPLICATIONS

Publications under this heading are divided into three categories. First, studies of the arms trade and military aid in general, their impact on international structures and processes, with some information also on the effects of both the senders and receivers of arms. Sellers and buyers, senders and receivers are dealt with in more detail in publications in the two other categories. In one, the policies of arms-exporting countries and the machinery for promoting arms sales are investigated. The local economic, political, and military impact of weapons transfers on receiver countries are considered in the third; publications dealing with the interrelationships between weapons transfers and domestic conflicts, political stability and economic development are also included in this category.

III.1 General implications of the arms trade and military assistance

84. Arms Trade and Transfer of Military Technology. Bulletin of Peace Proposals, vol. 8, No. 2, 1977, p. 99-192.

This extensive compilation of papers (most originally contributed to a Pugwash symposium in 1976) contains analyses of the role of military technology in arms production and its transfer to the Third World (Dieter Senghaas, Signe Landgren-Bäckström, Mary Kaldor, Ulrich Albrecht, Peter Lock and Herbert Wulf). Articles also deal with relationships between economic dependency, arms transfers and development in the Third World (Asbjørn Eide and Miles Wolpin); and contradictions between the proposed New International Economic Order and the existing world military order (Jan Øberg). The papers provide a comprehensive picture of the role, causes, and consequences of the transfer of military technology from the standpoint of dependency and development in the Third World. This issue of the Bulletin of Peace Proposals also gives extracts of various recent proposals to curtail international transfers of arms.

85. Frank, Lewis A., The arms trade in international relations. Washington, D.C., Fredrick A. Praeger Inc., 1969, 266 p.

The study discusses the conduct and channels of the arms trade, arms control, strategy, military and economic aid and the impact of defence spending on national economies, world trends in military expenditure in 1965-1968 and the causes and effects of their growth within societies and on international relations.

86. Harkavy, Robert E., The arms trade and international systems. Cambridge, Mass., MIT Press, 1975, 291 p.

This study adopts a structural scheme of analysis. It attempts to establish linkages between the supplier markets and the behaviour of suppliers on the one hand and donor-recipient relationships and transfer modes on the other. The problem of dependence versus autarky as a variable is investigated. The model of the relationship between the arms trade and systemic characteristics is based on data covering the periods before and after the Second World War. A survey of control schemes concludes the study.

87. Kalyadin, Alexander; Vaneev, Vladimir, Arms deliveries to developing countries. New Perspectives, vol. 2, no. 5, 1972.

The authors analyse the attitudes of socialist and capitalist States towards armed national liberation struggles, emphasizing that deliveries of military equipment to the Third World have quite distinct socio-political purposes and aims. They say that precise socio-political criteria, concrete historical analysis and a strictly differentiated approach are necessary in such studies.

88. Congress of the United States, 92nd Congress, First Session, Economic issues before the subcommittee on economy in government of the Joint Economic Committee. Washington, D.C., Government Printing Office, 1971, 435 p.

Economic impact and costs, and different types of benefits from the military programme are considered by a number of specialists, including Nicholas Katzenbach, Morton Halperin, William Fulbright, and Charles Wolf. The Chairman of the subcommittee was William Proxmire. Statistical breakdowns of military assistance to individual countries since 1950.

89. Leitenberg, Milton, Notes on the diversion of resources for military purposes in developing nations. Journal of Peace Research, vol. 13, no. 2, 1976, p. 111-116.

A comprehensive review of mainly United States sources which give information concerning the depletion of non-renewable resources in the manufacture of arms, the sale of arms from developed to developing countries, and the proportion of arms exports in relation to total exports and aid to the developing countries.

90. Luckham, Robin, Militarism: arms and the internationalization of capital. IDS Bulletin (Sussex), vol. 8, no. 3, 1977, p. 38-50.

The author constructs an analytical framework to explore relationships between military organization, technology and economic, political and social structure. In Luckham's view, Third World militarization is largely a consequence of armament dynamics and the development of arms economies in industrialized countries through the internationalization of capital also in the military sector. On the other hand, economic forces sustaining the arms race are modified by the fact that it is also an instrument of the States and ruling classes which exercise or aspire to hegemony within the international system. Given the importance of these processes, the author is surprised that they have received so little serious discussion and research.

91. Stanton, John; Pearton, Maurice, The international trade in arms, London, Praeger, 1972, 244 p.

A broad survey of the arms trade since the Second World War, which marked a change from private trade in arms to arms sales as a major feature in diplomatic life. The pattern of controls and the incentives in supplier nations are reviewed. Industrial competition between Europe and the United States is stressed as a major variable. Short case studies of different attempts to implement an international embargo refer to Portugal, South Africa, Nigeria (Biafra), Israel and Latin America.

92. Stockholm International Peace Research Institute, The arms trade with the Third World, Harmondsworth, Penguin 1975 (abridged and updated 1971, paperback published under the same title, Stockholm, Almqvist & Wiksell, 1971, 910 p).

This general outline of the arms trade stresses the increasing share of Third World countries. Confined to major weapons, the relative roles of major suppliers - United States, USSR, United Kingdom, France and the People's Republic of China - are considered. For large geographical regions, the pattern of recipients is outlined. Brief case studies present a multivariate pattern. Domestic defence production is also included, and various tables provide quick reference. The history of "conventional" arms control is followed by tentative suggestions for controlling the arms trade.

93. _____ . Arms trade registers. The arms trade with the Third World. Cambridge, Mass., London and Stockholm, Almqvist & Wiksell, 1975, 176 p.

Lists of all major arms supplies to 97 developing countries 1950-1974; provides information on deals, numbers of items transferred, brief comments on individual deals.

94. Thayer, George, The war business - the international trade in armaments, New York,

Simon & Schuster, 1969 (several translations).

A detailed account of the arms trade since the Second World War, with particular reference to private dealers. Information based on interviews with persons involved and on open sources given in journalistic style. Competition among supplier nations, the development of United States domination, governmental incentives to export, the appearance of socialist countries as suppliers during the 1950s.

95. United States Arms Control and Disarmament Agency, World military expenditures and arms trade 1963-1973, Washington, D.C., 1975, 123 p.

The previous annual publication World military expenditures has been expanded to include, in addition to two detailed tables on military expenditure, gross national products, population, and armed forces, also information on world arms trade by recipient countries and major suppliers, and on the arms trade by groups, regions and countries. Data on 132 countries.

96. Väyrynen, Raimo, Arms trade, military aid and arms production: perspectives of the history, the present situation and possibilities of control, in R. Weiler and V. Zsifkovits (eds.), Unterwegs zum Frieden. Vienna, Herder Verlag, 1973, p. 95-129.

The paper explores the arms trade, military aid and arms production as part of international structures and suggests that these factors reinforce inequalities and international dominance. Impact of the arms trade and military aid on domestic conflicts and foreign policy in Latin American and Asian countries. A typology of approaches to control of the arms trade is provided.

97. Øberg, Jan, Arms trade with the Third World as an aspect of imperialism. Journal of Peace Research, vol. 12, no. 3, 1975, p. 213-234.

The transfer of major weapons from centre to periphery countries 1950-1973. The power to supply weapons is strongly concentrated and relatively stable. The arms trade correlates closely with other aspects of international dominance. It is claimed that the arms trade will expand through military-industrial sub-imperialism, i.e. periphery countries will import sophisticated weapons simultaneously with the initiation of domestic arms production. This could lead to a new division of labour in world military-economics.

III.2 The role of sellers and senders in arms transfers

98. Albrecht, Ulrich; Sommer, Birgit, Deutsche Waffen für die Dritte Welt. Militärhilfe und Entwicklungspolitik. (German weapons for the Third World. Military assistance and development policy.) Rowohlt, Reinbek, 1972, 156 p.

This study provides a theoretical framework for the concept of military aid and its role in social change and development policy. The authors conclude that military assistance tends to distort economic development in the Third World. Case studies on Guinea, Chad and Portugal; a survey of West German military assistance and its objectives; the authors' data on military aid programmes by country and on number and types of weapon systems delivered to the Third World.

99. Gardan, Eric, Dossier A ... comme armes (File A ... for Arms), Paris 1975, 321 p.

Description of the French network for the sale of arms and the different sectors of the French arms industry. Numerous accounts of illegal transactions during the 1960s, including ones with dealers from several European countries.

100. Joshua, Wynfred; Stephen, Gilbert, Arms for the Third World: Soviet military aid diplomacy. Baltimore, The Johns Hopkins Press, 1969, 166 p.

The authors explore Soviet military and economic aid to each of the developing regions: Middle East, Africa, South and South-East Asia, Latin America. Relationships between military aid, economic aid, and trade, and the use of military aid to support wars of national liberation.

101. Haftendorn, Helga, Militärhilfe und Rüstungsexporte der BRD (Military assistance and arms exports of the FRG). Düsseldorf, Bertelsmann Universitätsverlag, 1971, 144 p.

The study examines the export of military material from the Federal Republic of Germany and its connections with NATO obligations. The main question is whether military aid and military exports support foreign policy aspirations or not. The conclusions are based on statistical material.

102. La France trafiquant d'armes (France as arms merchant), Paris 1974, 96 p.

A survey of French arms exports is provided in this brochure prepared by the Centre for Information and Co-ordination of Non-Violent Action. Short bibliography, and a list of French firms involved in military production for export.

103. Klare, Michael T., Arms and power; The political economy of United States weapons sales to Latin America. NACLA's Latin America & Empire Report, vol. IX, no. 2, March 1975, 32 p.

United States arms sales policy in Latin America, politics of the arms trade, and forces underlying the current export drive are examined. Before his analysis of strategic, economic and political factors underlying arms transfers, the author criticizes the "bogus analysis fabricated by industry officials and their government allies". Detailed tables of major arms transfers to Latin America, military sales 1950-1974, leading weapon exporters, and a selected bibliography.

104. Lock, Peter; Wulf, Herbert, Deutsche Rüstungsexporte trotz Beschränkungen: Folgen für die Bundesrepublik und die Dritte Welt (German arms exports despite limitations; Consequences for the FRG and the Third World), Friedensanalysen für Theorie und Praxis, no. 3, Frankfurt 1976, p. 93-100.

Arms producers of the Federal Republic of Germany - despite the official policy of restricting arms exports - have maintained their share in transferring arms to Third World countries and in establishing production facilities abroad to circumvent export controls. In the long run, arms transfers will have negative consequences not only for development in the recipient countries but also for the home economy.

105. Paul, Roland A., American military commitments abroad. New Brunswick, N.J., Rutgers University Press, 1973, 237 p.

A summary of United States military involvement and commitments abroad: besides NATO countries, a detailed picture is given of involvement in Taiwan, Japan, Laos, Morocco and others. In connection with NATO, the author examines at length the question of troop reductions, cost saving and balance of payments. He considers how various agreements can best serve American national interests and the extent to which government policy influences other governments.

106. Stein, Nancy; Klare, Michael, Merchants of repression. United States police exports to the Third World. NACLA's Latin America Report, July-August 1976, p. 31-38.

Arms sales to police forces in the Third World represent only a small percentage of total United States weapons exports, but probably have a greater impact on the day-to-day lives of people in developing countries than regular military sales. Country-by-country tables show such exports from 1973 to 1976, giving quantity, manufacturer and product, exporter, date of licence and recipient.

107. Vincineau, Michel, La Belgique et commerce des armes (Belgium and the arms trade), Brussels 1974, 286 p.

The acceleration of a world-wide arms race leads to the development of more sophisticated weapons with increased destructive power. Belgium, although a small country, is heavily involved in the arms trade. The legal situation and administrative practices related to the arms trade are described in detail. Transactions with South Africa, Portugal, Brazil and Indo-China are given as examples. A history of the parliamentary and political background is followed by a detailed list of Belgian companies involved in arms manufacture.

III. 3 Impact of arms transfers on receiving countries

108. Albrecht, Ulrich; Ernst, Dieter; Lock, Peter;

Wulf, Herbert, Rüstung und Unterentwicklung. Iran, Indien, Griechenland/Türkei: Die verschärfte Militarisierung, (Armament and underdevelopment. Iran, India, Greece/Turkey: intensified militarization), Reinbek, Rowohlt, 1976, 245 p.

Armaments and militarism are not only important in international relations, but also a constituent element in the economic, social and political development of the Third World. The transfer of arms and especially the production of arms in developing countries perpetuate underdevelopment and dependence, structuring the industrial pattern. A survey of arms production in developing countries and a historical analysis are given; three case studies on the results of armament dynamics in Iran, India and Greece/Turkey. A research bibliography is also included.

109. Antola, Esko, The roots of domestic military interventions in Black Africa. Instant Research on Peace and Violence, vol. 5, no. 4, 1975, p. 207-221.

The author argues in his empirical study of 52 military coups d'état in Black Africa that it is erroneous to consider these coups as a problem of domestic civil-military relations; they should rather be seen in the context of neo-colonial policies. Special attention is given to the international economic position of the countries concerned, and to the activities in them of transnational corporations.

110. Burrell, R.M.; Cottrell, A.J., Iran, Afghanistan, Pakistan: tensions and dilemmas. Beverly Hills and London 1974, 68 p.

This volume of the Washington Papers series published by the Center for Strategic and International Studies of Georgetown University, provides a comprehensive account of vested interests affecting policies, and discusses prospects for military alliances and foreign power involvement.

111. Barang, Marcel, L'Iran: Renaissance d'un empire (Iran: Rebirth of an empire). Le Monde diplomatique. May 1975, p. 20-24.

A comprehensive account of the process of militarization in Iran. Involvement of foreign personnel in military training, arms production and police support.

112. Childs, Dennis; Kidron, Michael, India, the USSR and the MIG project. Economic and Political Weekly, vol. VIII, no. 38, September 1973, p. 1721-1728.

The article states that the Indo-Soviet MIG production programme in India has not been a success. As the MIG is inferior in performance to many of Pakistan's aircraft, its production in India would be justified only if it could be manufactured in large numbers and at low prices. But the plane was not cheap, even in terms of foreign exchange, was not produced in large numbers, production was running behind schedule, and the aircraft was still more Russian-made than Indian-made.

113. Crocker, Chester A., Military dependence: the colonial legacy in Africa. The Journal of Modern African Studies, vol. 12, no. 2, 1974, p. 265-286.

African dependence has an important military aspect and changes in African forces and external strategic interests affect contemporary international relations. The Africanization of the colonial armies reflected ideas of planners in Britain and France. In an analysis of the military transfer of power, imperial disengagement and national institution-building are integral parts of the same process. Whereas France and Britain had traditionally absorbed troops from Africa and Asia for their armies in Europe, the post-war period has been characterized by net imports of white manpower for the new national armies in Africa.

114. Eide, Asbjørn, The transfer of arms to Third World countries and their internal uses. International Social Science Journal, vol. XXVIII, no. 2, 1976, p. 307-325.

The legitimate right of Third World countries to defend themselves against external threat and the necessity of military aid for armed liberation struggles are not challenged. But the militarization of many developing countries mainly serves for internal repression: arms imports and the production of arms are likely to increase the structural dependence of Third World countries. Therefore developing countries should opt for a different kind of armed force that is not dependent upon the industrialized countries, and they should press much more strongly for global disarmament.

115. Loveday, Douglas F., The role of US military bases in the Philippine economy. Prepared for Office of the Assistant Secretary of Defense, International Security Affairs. Santa Monica, California, Rand Corp., 1971, 60 p.

Income generated by the United States bases was about 9.6 per cent of the Philippine GNP in 1967. While these estimates of the local economic impact of the bases are not projections of actual income losses to be expected should they be removed, the study suggests that this loss of dollar earnings, unless compensated by gains elsewhere, might have a significant effect on the Philippine balance of payments and terms of trade. Major adjustments of economic activities could become necessary.

116. Misra, K. P., International politics in the Indian Ocean. Orbis, vol. XVIII, no. 4, 1975, p. 1088-1108.

The notion of a "power vacuum" in the Indian Ocean is criticized as an outgrowth of the traditional theory of the balance of power, suggesting that the nations of Asia and Africa bordering the Indian Ocean are unable to defend themselves. The efforts of the littoral States to establish the Indian Ocean as a peace zone, the reactions of the super-powers, United States proposals to build a base at Diego Garcia are examined, and strategies to keep foreign powers out of the area are discussed.

117. Nafziger, Wayne E., The political economy of disintegration in Nigeria. Journal of Modern African Studies, vol. 11, no. 4, 1973, p. 505-536.

Conflicts at different levels in Nigeria are related to political and economic influences from abroad. The increase of military expenditure on continuous increases in force levels and on the modernization of equipment is analysed.

118. Pauker, G. J. et al., In search of self-reliance: US security assistance to the Third World under the Nixon doctrine. Rand Corp., R-1092-ARPA, June 1973, 66 p.

Elaborating the Nixon doctrine as far as United States forces planning is concerned, the study stresses the need for "self-reliance" among Third World armed forces. These do not need expensive and complex weapon systems, but intermediate technologies. Self-reliance, and the "unbroken record of successes in counter-insurgency operations" in Indonesia are possible in other Third World countries, and especially in Greece and Turkey on NATO's southern flank.

119. Stockholm International Peace Research Institute (SIPRI), Southern Africa. The escalation of a conflict. A politico-military study. New York, London & Stockholm, Praeger Publishers, Almqvist & Wiksell, 1976, x + 235 p.

The conflicts in Southern Africa, including the former Portuguese colonies. The local and international determinants of these conflicts are discussed. One section is devoted to an investigation of the military strength of the Republic of South Africa and Rhodesia, and of South Africa's strategic importance to the West. Tables on major arms imports into South Africa (1950-1975), Rhodesia and Portugal, and a bibliography.

120. Tahtinen, Dale R., Arms in the Persian Gulf. Washington, D. C., American Enterprise Institute, 1974, 31 p.

No. 10 of the Foreign Affairs Studies published by the American Enterprise Institute for Public Policy Research provides a detailed comparative account of the military build-up in the Gulf area and American involvement there. A settlement of the Arab-Israel conflict is seen as a prerequisite for a stable situation within the Gulf.

121. Technologie und Politik. (Technology and politics), Aktuell-Magazin No. 4, Reinbek, Rowohlt, 1976, 180 p.

All articles in this volume are concerned with armaments and weapons technology: napalm, SALT II, arms exports, nuclear technology (especially the transfer of a complete nuclear fuel cycle from the FRG to Brazil), and private security organizations. A research guide (prepared by an IPRA study group) to the literature on arms and armed forces, and an appreciation of the standard handbooks (IISS and SIPRI) are included.

122. Wolpin, Miles D., Military aid and counter-revolution in the Third World, Lexington, Mass., Toronto & London, Lexington Books, 1972, 327 p.

An assessment of United States military aid as an instrument of foreign policy for influencing the internal politics of developing countries, concentrating on military training rather than the transfer of weapons. The traditional justifications for training programmes (to train foreign military men in handling equipment) are confronted with the objectives of the military assistance training programme (policy suggestions and promotion of particular development ideology). The testimony of officials, congressmen, officers, and scholars in congressional hearings are excerpted and summarized. Index and bibliography.

123. Øberg, Jan, Third World armament: Domestic arms production in Israel, South Africa, Brazil, Argentina and India, 1950-1975. Instant Research on Peace and Violence, vol. 5, no. 4, 1975, p.222-239.

A detailed survey of domestic arms production in the Third World which has assumed extensive proportions in some countries. These are usually also significant importers of arms from the major powers. The article tries to see whether the five countries display sub-imperialist behaviour patterns. The author suggests ways of integrating different research approaches to the problem of domestic arms production in the Third World.

IV.   MILITARY REGIMES IN THE THIRD WORLD
       AND THEIR IMPACT ON SOCIETY

The studies listed are mainly concerned with the relations between the army and the political élite in developing countries. A frequent theme is the control of political life by the military establishment, often after a coup d'état. Studies analysing, qualitatively or quantitatively, the background and roots of military interventions into political life are mostly excluded, since the main concern is with the political and economic aspects of military regimes in the Third World. Studies included are, as a rule, more interested in the domestic than in the external aspects of military regimes.

124. Bahiana, Henrique Paulo, As forces armades e o desinvolvimiento do Brasil (The armed forces and underdevelopment in Brazil), Rio de Janeiro, 1974, 202 p.

A semi-official account of the Brazilian armed

forces with particular reference to activities traditionally considered civilian.

125. Bienen, Henry (ed.), The military and modernization. Chicago, 1971.

The role of the military in modernization in developing countries; essays mostly based on political sociology. The alleged role of the military as a progressive force in developing countries is criticized, the conclusions reached pointing the opposite way.

126. Decalo, Samuel, Military coups and military regimes in Africa. The Journal of Modern African Studies, vol. II, no. 1, 1973, p. 105-127.

Many recent studies on coups d'état in Africa and on the political role of African armies are reviewed and criticized, especially for their lack of detailed case studies based on field work. More recent studies are examined under three headings: political sociology and historiography, the preconditions for military interventions, and the military as rulers.

127. Doorn, Jacques van (ed.), Military profession and military regimes, The Hague & Paris, Humanities, 1969, 304 p.

In three sociological contributions on various parts of the world (mainly Third World but also some socialist countries), political control by the armed forces and reasons for military interventions are analysed.

128. Eleazu, Uma O., The role of the army in African politics. A reconsideration of existing theories and practices. Journal of Developing Areas, no. 7, 1973, p. 265-286.

In contrast to the existing schools of thought regarding military intervention as a process of nation-building, a neglected aspect of the role of the military in Africa is examined: their foreign origin and support.

129. Gott, Richard, Rural guerillas in Latin America, Harmondsworth, Penguin, 1973, 637 p.

A detailed account of Latin American rural guerillas in the 1960s, including defeat in Bolivia and Ché Guevara's death in 1967. The author was local correspondent of a British newspaper and provides the testimony of many eye-witnesses.

130. Gutteridge, W.F., Military regimes in Africa; Studies in African history, London 1975, 195 p.

As a frequent writer on the role of the military particularly in former British possessions, Gutteridge gives a detailed and well-informed account of military interventions in Ghana, Nigeria, Uganda and the Sudan; Zaire and Dahomey (Benin), former Belgian and French territories, are also covered. Sociological, Bureaucratic and promotion problems within African military establishments as compared to British Army practice are analysed in detail. Generally he feels that the military are unable to handle the political problems of present-day Africa, because of the lack of clear-cut political objectives.

131. Joxe, Alain, Las fuerzas armadas en el sistema politico de Chile, (The armed forces in the Chilean political system), Santiago de Chile, 1970, 176 p.

Part One covers the history of the Chilean armed forces and their role in the political process. Part Two analyses their political role on a comparative basis, with particular reference to foreign aid and military transfers. The disappearance of the traditional middle class is considered a key variable in assessing future developments.

132. Kennedy, Gavin, The military in the Third World, London, Duckworth, 1974, 368 p.

In seventeen chapters, various hypotheses about causal links in military interventions in developing countries are tested by case studies, cross-national statistical analysis, and qualitative evaluation. Low income countries experience military intervention relatively more often. Violence is not a consequence of military intervention. Interventions in Sierra Leone, Ghana, Nigeria, Indonesia, Pakistan, Egypt, Syria and Iraq are discussed. Mexico, Israel and Turkey are given as typical cases of non-intervention explained by the absence of a "legitimacy crisis". Military expenditure does not a priori represent a burden inhibiting economic growth. The Biafran War "imposed economic discipline ... and the emergency provided the kind of stimulus to economic nation-building that seven years of independence had failed to produce". (p. 207) A positive link between local arms manufacture and industrial development is posited.

133. Lindenberg, Klaus, Fuerzas armades y politica en America Latina; Bibliografia selecta, (The armed forces and politics in Latin America. A selected bibliography), Santiago de Chile 1972, 199 p.

This bibliography contains over 1,000 titles on the role of the armed forces in Latin America; country and author index.

134. Mazrui, Ali A., The lumpen proletariat and the lumpen militariat: African soldiers as a new political class. Political Studies, vol. XXI, no. 1, 1973, p. 1-12.

Starting from the premise of modernization, the military is seen as a key group for social and economic change. They are considered as a non-élite (lumpen-militariat), a class of semi-organized, rugged and semi-literate soldiery. The control, not of the means of production, but of the means of destruction has been the decisive political force in the history of independent Africa.

135. Mirsky, Grigory I., The Third World. Society, power, army. Moscow, Nauka Publishers. 1976, 408 p.

G. I. Mirsky, using Marxist-Leninist methodology, considers the preconditions for the army's emergence on the political arena; the causes of coups d'états and the aims of the military; the military in power; the military and revolutionary democracy. He argues that the army does not live in a vacuum but in the midst of society, seething with class struggle. That is why the claim of most military rulers that they are "governing without politics" is at best hollow, and the ruling military élite turns into a bureaucratic military anti-national caste. On the other hand, the military can also play a progressive role in the development of society. Mirsky also discusses external determinants of military rule and observes, for example, that the increased political role of the army does not go unnoticed in neo-colonialist circles, which try to spread their influence among officers in young States.

136. Mercier Vega, Luis (ed.), Fuerzas armadas, poder y cambio, (The armed forces; power and change), Caracas, 1971, 364 p.

Essays on the role of the military in the history of Latin America; case studies on Mexico, Peru, Argentina, Uruguay and Bolivia. A systematic framework presented by Oscar Cuéllar.

137. Schmittar, Philippe (ed.), Military rule in Latin America. Function, consequences and perspectives. Beverly Hills & London, Sage Publications, 1973, 322 p.

Contributions by Rouquié, Weaver, Schmitter, Kemp and Kurth provide a broad range of cross-national comparisons of socio-political structures in Latin American countries. Several functional hypotheses on the role of the military are tested, employing statistical analysis among other methods.

138. Stepan, Alfred C., The military in politics, changing patterns in Brazil, Princeton, 1971, 313 p.

Civil-military relations in Brazil are traced back to the time of the United States-Brazilian military alliance during the Second World War. A detailed analysis of the social and political background of the officer corps. Institutional antecedents to military takeover described include the role of the Escola Superior de Guerra in preparing a civil-military élite for government: comprehensive data and practical research advice.

V. MILITARY R&D (RESEARCH AND DEVELOPMENT) AND ITS IMPACT ON SCIENTIFIC INSTITUTIONS

The contributions in this section are few, but representative of the studies dealing with military

R&D and its impact on society and scientific institutions. There are some studies dealing with the general development of military research or with advances in special sectors like operations research, but only a few systematically explore the consequences of this sort of research.

139. Albrecht, Ulrich, Prioritäten in der Rüstungsforschung (Priorities in armament research), in Wolfgang Port (ed.), Wissenschaftspolitik - von wem, für wen, wie? Prioritäten in der Forschungsplanung, (Science policy - by whom, for whom, how? Priorities in research planning). Munich, Carl Hanser Verlag, 1973, p. 118-143.

The author explores the extent of military R&D in the Federal Republic of Germany and provides some explanations for the increase in such spending, relating military R&D to more general trends in armament dynamics. He considers the roles played by the military establishment, the State and industry in the formation of military R&D policies in the Federal Republic.

140. Annerstedt, Jan, et al., Datorer och politik. Studier i en ny tekniks politiska effekter på det svenska samhället. (Data and politics. Studies on the political effects of new technology on Swedish society). Kristianstad, Bo Cavefors Bokförlag, 1970, 224 p.

How closely military and civilian data registers are integrated and the extent to which the needs of the military have shaped the development of data systems in general. Case studies allow the authors to conclude that the degree of integration is fairly high and that the military establishment has had a key role in introducing data registers and systems in Sweden in the 1950s. Since then, it has pioneered their application.

141. Buzujev, V. M.; Pavlicenko, V. P., Učenye v bor'be za mir i progress. Iz istorii Pagouškogo dviženija (Scientists fighting for peace and progress. From the history of the Pugwash movement). Moscow, Izdatel'stvo, Nauka, 1967.

The book contains much factual material about the activities of international and national organizations of scientists fighting for the peaceful use of science and international security, and in particular, the Pugwash movement.

142. Coman, Ion, Revolutia stiintifică si tehnică si implicatiile lor în domeniul militar. (The scientifico-technical revolution and its military implications.) Bucharest, Editura Politica, 1972, 255 p.

The author, a well-known specialist, reviews the repercussions of the scientifico-technical revolution on military matters - primarily on the arms race.

143. Kaldor, Mary, European defence industries - national and international implications. ISIO Monographs, first series, no. 8, University of Sussex 1972, 79 p.

A detailed analysis of the structure and character of defence production and exports in Western Europe, including costs, technological advance and the financial structure of the arms market. Crucial role of military R&D in shaping most of the components of domestic defence markets and transnational collaboration projects.

144. Klare, Michael, War without end. American planning for the next Vietnams. New York, Vintage Books, 1972, 464 p.

The development of United States military strategy vis-à-vis the Third World, related research activities, existing research centres, counter-insurgency research networks and "social systems engineering" for counter-insurgency purposes. Klare's is probably the most detailed single analysis of this subject.

145. Kuczynski, Jürgen, Wissenschaft und Rüstung, (Science and armament) Jahrbuch für Wirtschaftsgeschichte 1973, Part 1, Berlin 1973.

The author examines the share of armament in GNP and in R&D expenditure, the role of scientists in the military-industrial complex in imperialist countries, the situation of basic and military research. The stimulating effect of disarmament on the scientific-economic revolution and the latter's influence on military and civil industry are also discussed.

146. Leitenberg, Milton, Vetenskapen och dagens militära teknofogi (Science and the military technology of today). Stockholm, Internationella studier, no. 9, 1972, 46 p.

The role of military R&D in the development of military technology, uses of this technology in the Second World War and in Viet Nam. The author gives a vivid picture of the dynamics of the present military technology and of its relations to applied and basic research. A statistical appendix and a lengthy bibliography. The main thesis is that military R&D is an essential factor in fuelling the qualitative arms race.

147. Nelkin, Dorothy, The university and military research; moral politics at MIT. Ithaca, Cornell University Press, 1972, 195 p.

A case study of the Massachusetts Institute of Technology's handling of the controversy over government-sponsored research in its instrumentation laboratory. Nelkin examines the attitudes of the university to national priorities and its relations with defence establishments, military objectives and politics. The political and moral arguments for the conversion of military R&D to civilian research purposes are discussed.

148. Nelson, Richard R., Impact of disarmament on research and development, in Benoit, Emile

and Boulding, Kenneth (ed.), Disarmament and the economy. New York, Harper & Row, 1964, p. 112-130.

The author concludes, after a detailed analysis, that the growth of military and space R&D has significantly retarded the growth of civilian R&D, hence a significant decrease in the military R&D funds could be used with large benefit to society. R&D resources released by disarmament could be used to expand foreign aid programmes. Disarmament would also provide an unmatched opportunity to review public policies toward non-military R&D, and to foster civilian R&D where private incentives and financial capacities are weak, e.g. for housing and urban transport.

149. Rosenbluth, Gideon, The effect of disarmament on research and development in Canada, Proceedings of the International Peace Research Association Inaugural Conference. Assen, Van Gorcum, 1966, p. 247-269.

The extent and character of R&D spending in Canada, benefits which could follow disarmament. Little information on military R&D as such in Canada, but considerable attention to transition problems. Unless disarmament is associated with depression, no real shortage of demand for skilled workers should result from the curtailment of defence research. The author points out that military research seldom has significant civilian applications.

150. Rotblat, J., Scientists in the quest for peace. A history of the Pugwash Conference. Cambridge, Mass., The MIT Press, 1972, 399 p.

An account by the former Secretary-General of the Pugwash Conference, its origin, organization, and activities since 1957. Its influence in shaping attitudes in the academic community and on the arms control policies of the major military powers. A supplement for the years 1972-1977 has been published by Rotblat in Pugwash Newsletter, Special Issue, May 1977, 72 p.

151. Stockholm International Peace Research Institute (SIPRI), Resources devoted to military research and development, Stockholm, Almqvist & Wiksell, 1972, 112 p.

A comprehensive mapping of resources devoted to military R&D in 22 major spending countries. Estimates of both world-wide and national levels of military R&D, their share of total government R&D outlay, and of total military spending. Trends in military R&D spending in different countries 1955-1971. This useful SIPRI publication is in fact the first comprehensive effort to cover world trends in military R&D spending.

152. Vaneev, Vladimir; Tomilin, Yuri; Glasov, Victor, Scientific and technological progress and disarmament. International détente and disarmament. Contributions by Finnish and Soviet scholars.

Tampere Peace Research Institute, Helsinki 1977, p. 134-160.

Main trends in scientific and technological development, and their impact on the arms race and disarmament problems. Problems of prohibiting new types and systems of weapons of mass destruction and the use of the environment for military purposes.

153. Väyrynen, Raimo, Sotilaallinen tutkimus Suomessa (Military research in Finland), in Kettil Bruun et al., (eds.), Tiedepolitiikka ja tutkijan vastuu (Science policy and the responsibility of scientists). Helsinki, Tammi, 1976, p. 258-279.

The creation of State bodies to co-ordinate military-oriented research in Finland and efforts to involve university research in this general scheme. The extent and general organization of military research, impact of government-financed military R&D on the academic community and on the present and future patterns of military spending in Finland.

154. York, Herbert, The advisors. Oppenheimer, Teller and the superbomb. San Francisco, W. H. Freeman and Co., 1976, 175 p.

A participant's view of the development of the atomic bomb, mainly in the United States but also in the Soviet Union. The author describes relations between scientists and policy-makers and shows how profoundly both are affected. Effects on the structure of the scientific community, and resulting divisions and debates. Policy-makers seem better able to preserve their integrity; scientists find their careers partly decided by policy-makers, and hence are in a far more vulnerable position.

155. _____, Greb, Allen, Military research and development: a post-war history. Bulletin of the Atomic Scientists, vol. 33, no. 1, 1977, p. 13-26.

The authors explore in considerable detail the organization of military research and development in the United States since the Second World War and schedule the various phases of military R&D: 1945-1950, demobilization and uncertainty; 1950-1953, some remobilization after the first Soviet atomic bomb and the Korean War; 1953-1958, further remobilization and reorganization in response to a new military strategy; 1957-1977, the launching of the Soviet Sputnik brought military R&D qualitatively and quantitatively to new levels. This period also saw the decline and demise of the President's Science Advisory Committee. This, according to the authors, has eliminated the only effective counter-force to the military R&D administration.

VI. CONSEQUENCES OF DISARMAMENT AND OF THE ARMS RACE FOR THE INTERNATIONAL SYSTEM AND ITS PROCESSES

This part of the bibliography deals with studies which explore consequences of the arms race and of disarmament from the standpoint of international functional, geographic, or politico-legal aspects. The first section refers to general connections between the arms race and disarmament on the one hand, and, on the other, the economic and socio-political structure of the world, and future prospects. Some of the studies exceed the scope of this chapter and have already been listed elsewhere. The second section deals primarily with connections between disarmament and international legal-political structures. The socialist countries figure largely since they favour a generalist approach, whereas specific, quantitative studies are more in favour in the West.

VI. 1 Arms race, disarmament and international processes

156. Benoit, Emile, Disarmament and world economic interdependence. Oslo, Universitetsforlaget, New York/London, Columbia University Press, 1967, 260 p.

Papers prepared for the Conference on Economic Aspects of World Disarmament and Interdependence, held in Oslo in August 1965. Economic considerations which tend to shape arms control and disarmament policies in the Soviet Union, China, the United Kingdom and Norway. Consequences of disarmament for atomic and space industries, and for R&D. Economic structures and dynamics of an "interdependent world", East-West relations, structure of an international division of labour.

157. Gyovai, Gyula; Kozma, Ferenc; Sütő, Otto; Tolnai, László, Tudományos Konferencia a nemzetközi enyhülés és a keletnyugati kapcsolatck fejlődésének kilátásairól. (Scientific conference on the perspectives of international détente and the development of East-West relations), Külpolitika, vol. 1976, no. 1, p. 105-118.

Main topics discussed at the Tihany Conference in September 1975: Perspectives of development in the political situation of Europe (results, problems and possibilities in connection with international détente. European security and military détente); the role of the development of Soviet-United States relations in détente and disarmament. Military-political question of international détente: military détente, SALT, negotiations on the reduction of armed forces and armaments in Central Europe, problems of military integration in Western Europe; influence of the world economic situation on détente.

158. Ivanov, K.; Bacanov, B., Vzglad v zavtra (A look at tomorrow), Moscow, Izdatel'stvo Meždunarodnye Otnošenija, 1964.

New possibilities created by modern science and technology. Prospects for the development of world productive forces and ways of overcoming the backwardness of economically underdeveloped countries. The problem is discussed in the context of general and complete disarmament.

159. Janku, V. Mírové soužití - reálný faktor mezinárodních vztahu (Peaceful coexistence - a real factor of international relations), Nová mysl (New mind), 2, 1973, p. 221-234.

Changes in post-war developments in international relations. The author says imperialism had to take account of reality and the new balance of forces. Détente does not influence the class struggle, which forms a basis of existing international relations. However, the centre of struggle is increasingly shifting to economic and ideological grounds.

160. Kalyadin, A. N., Bor'ba za razoruženie: Novye perspektivy (The struggle for disarmament: New perspectives). Mirovaja ékonomika i meždunarodnye otnošenija, Moscow, No. 11, 1974, p. 3-14. (Also published in Instant Research on Peace and Violence, no. 1, 1975, p. 24-34.)

Implications of international détente in solving arms limitation problems. Various partial measures taken during the last 15 years are assessed. All the existing treaties, agreements and other arrangements are considered by the author as an embryo for an international system of arms control. Difficulties, opportunities, and possible policies are examined in the context of a deepening and widening international détente.

161. _____, Kade, Gerhard; Détente and disarmament. Problems and perspectives. Vienna, International Institute for Peace, 1976, 157 p.

Papers contributed to various symposia by the International Institute for Peace in 1975-1976, covering the nature and scale of the modern arms race, relations between détente and disarmament, specific problems of armament limitation and disarmament (including the conversion of military R&D, the reduction of military budgets, present arms control negotiations, and ideological and scientifico-technical aspects of the arms race and disarmament). Authors from both socialist and market-economy countries. The book also contains documents of public forums on disarmament during 1975-1976.

162. Kirilov, Ognjan, Razor'zavane. Aktualni problemi (Disarmament: Current problems). Sofia, Partizadt, 1975, 191 p.

The essence of disarmament - scientific questions which the author considers the most significant or whose solution offers the greatest prospects.

The place, importance and role of disarmament in modern international development, and ways of solving the problems in question.

163. Pirityi, Sándor, A leszerelés (Disarmament) Kiádó, Budapest, 1975, Zrinyi, 416 p. (Bib. p. 406-407).

Topics include: disarmament in relation to politics, war, armament and détente; history of disarmament up to 1945; disarmament bodies and agreements, 1945-1975; the positions and actions of the great powers on the question of disarmament; disarmament negotiations and agreements: nuclear disarmament, biological and chemical weapons, demilitarization of outer space and the sea bed, "conventional" disarmament; the Soviet Union and the United States for disarmament: SALT and other agreements; Europe and disarmament: NATO, Warsaw Treaty, the two German States and disarmament, the connection between European security and the Vienna talks on arms reduction with disarmament; calendar of events (1945-1975) and bibliography on disarmament.

164. Rattinger, Johannes, Rüstungsdynamik im internationalen System. Mathematische Reaktions-modelle für Rüstungswettläufe und die Probleme ihrer Anwendung (Armaments dynamics in the international system. Mathematical reaction models for arms race and problems of their application). München, R. Oldenbourh Verlag, 1975, 473 p.

Mainly mathematical analyses of the arms race; various models compared. Relations between the arms race and the occurrence of wars, comparative shares of military expenditure in State budgets and GNP; various aspects of the relations between armaments and international processes.

165. Stockholm International Peace Research Institute (SIPRI), Oil and security. A SIPRI monograph. New York and Stockholm, Humanities Press and Almqvist & Wiksell International, 1974, 197 p.

Oil supply, dependence patterns and alternative sources of energy. The 1973 embargo, territorial disputes related to oil, Washington Energy Conference of February 1974. Analyses of arms transfers to oil-producing countries and their impact on local society. It is shown in a relatively detailed manner that oil is of special military importance, and that military considerations have an undeniable impact on the world's energy economy.

166. Svetlov, A., Problema razoruženija i razrjadka meždunarodnoj naprjažennosti. (The disarmament problem and international détente.) Moscow, Politizdat, 1975.

The author considers major arms limitation issues in relation to détente in international relations. The growing significance of international détente for the success of disarmament.

167. Verona, Sergiu, Dezarmarea si relatiile

internationale, (Disarmament and international relations), Bucharest, Editura Militara, 1976, 300 p.

Background of the nuclear arms race and the strategic and military doctrines and concepts that govern it. While rejecting the theory of "the balance of terror" as a means of ensuring international stability, the author points to the advantages offered by nuclear disarmament.

VI.2 Socio-legal aspects of disarmament and the arms race

168. Bogdanov, O. V., Razoruženie - garantija mira (Meždunarodnopravovye aspekty) (Disarmament - A guarantee for peace (International law aspects)). Moscow, Izdatel'stvo Meždunarodnye Otnošenija, 1972.

International legal aspects of specific steps in disarmament (e. g. non-proliferation of nuclear weapons, nuclear test ban, chemical and bacteriological disarmament, general and complete disarmament). The growing role of international law in disarmement. A forecast of the likely development of legal norms and principles in relation to arms limitation and disarmament.

169. Buza, Laszlo, A Leszerelés és a nemzetközi jogi törvényesség. Magyar Jog (Disarmament and international law). Hungarian Law, no. 6, 1963, p. 246-252.

Anti-war activity of the League of Nations between the two world wars; disarmament attempts and the Cold War after the second; Soviet initiative in 1959 for general and complete disarmament, and its influence; the Eighteen-Nation Committee on Disarmament, 1959-1963; basic questions of disarmament in international law.

170. Čebiš, V., K otázce obecného zákazu používáníplynu v ozbrojených konfliktech (The problem of general prohibition of the usage of gas in armed conflicts), Casopis pro mezinárodní právo (Czechoslovak Journal for International Law), 2, 1966, p. 107-121.

History of the prohibition of chemical warfare; the Geneva Protocol of 1925 and its significance; further extension of the prohibition of chemical warfare; prohibition of the use of gas in armed conflicts as a universal norm of international customary law; critique of some aspects of the United States' apology in connection with the use of gas in Viet Nam.

171. Disarmament, détente and development. Papers from the IPRA Disarmament Study Group. Instant Research on Peace and Violence, vol. 6, no. 1-2, 1976, 92 p.

This special issue (eight articles) includes articles by Ulrich Anbrecht (Arms trade with the Third World and domestic arms production) and

Asbjørn Eide and Pertti Joenniemi (development and control possibilities of conventional weapons). Recent developments in conventional weapons (e.g. incendiary weapons, small-calibre projectiles, blast, fragmentation and time-delay weapons) have increased human suffering in war, and their control has become an increasingly urgent issue.

172. Gilas, J., O istocie prawnej powszechnego i calkowitego rozbrojenia (On the legal essence of universal and complete disarmament), Sprawy Miedzynarodowe, no. 5, 1963.

The author states that international law has historically regarded disarmament as a postulate of legal doctrine, but he believes that it should be studied primarily from the political point of view. The article contains a detailed analysis of the disarmament problem in the light of the United Nations Charter. On the basis of the documents adopted by them in the General Assembly, the Member States have established a new legal principle - the principle of universal and complete disarmament. This, in turn, has been confirmed in many bilateral agreements between States. The article is based on extensive bibliographical material.

173. Kopal, V., Právní rezim oblasti vyhrazených mírovým účelúm (Legal status of areas reserved for peaceful purposes), Časopis pro mezinárodní právo, (Czechoslovak Journal for International Law), no. 3, 1966, p. 205-222.

Topics include: efforts to create nuclear-free zones; the Antarctic Treaty as the first successful example of conferring a peaceful status on a particular area; the attempt to create a peaceful status for outer space; conditions for the conclusion of the treaty regarding the peaceful exploration of the moon and other celestial bodies.

174. Luard, Evan, The control of the sea bed. A new international issue. London, Heinemann, 1974, 309 p.

A general account of the uses and control of the sea bed which also considers efforts to militarize the sea bed and the dangers that it involves (p. 49-60). The author discusses the debate on the demilitarization of the sea bed (p. 97-112) and certain aspects of it, viz. the scope and extent of the 1972 Treaty banning the emplacement of nuclear weapons or other weapons of mass destruction on the sea bed and subsoil thereof. He also considers the enforcement and verification of this Treaty.

175. Nándori, Pál, A leszerelés nemzetközi jogi és egyéb kérdései (International legal and other questions of disarmament), Jogi Tájékoztató, 1963, p. 61-93.

The article reviews the concept and classifications of disarmament; first attempts at The Hague conferences; inter-war disarmament activity of the League of Nations; disarmament and the United Nations Charter; disarmament negotiations 1945 to 1959; the campaign for general and complete disarmament 1959 to 1963; unilateral disarmament measures by the Soviet Union and the socialist countries; financial and economic consequences of disarmament; international legal prohibition of weapons of mass destruction; the significance of the Moscow Partial Nuclear Test-Ban Treaty.

176. Penkov, Sava; 25 godini s'ščestvuvane na OON i razor'žavaneto (Ocenki i perspektivi) (The twenty-fifth anniversary of the United Nations and disarmament (assessments and perspectives)). Pravna Mis'l (Sofia), no. 5, 1971, p. 98-103.

The article examines the 25-year period during which the United Nations have worked for disarmament. The first years (1945-1960) were characterized by fruitless negotiations and attempts to implement certain articles. The second period, beginning in 1960, saw numerous international treaties on disarmament. Certain of the more significant drafts tabled by the USSR and the socialist countries for discussions at the United Nations are enumerated. It is stressed that the activity of the United Nations during the Disarmament Decade (1970-1979) must rely mainly on the efforts of the socialist and peace-loving powers throughout the world.

177. _____, Meždunarodnopravni problemi na razor'žavaneto (Problems of disarmament in international law), Sofia, Nauka i iskusstvo, 1966, 104 p.

This book is in two parts. The first deals with three types of weapons of mass destruction, and the relevant international customary law is analysed in detail - including international agreements (1899-1945) to ban the use of chemical, bacteriological and nuclear weapons. The second is devoted to the Moscow Partial Test Ban Treaty, legal questions, theoretical and practical, obligations undertaken, the right of joining or abrogating the Treaty, etc. Special attention is given to the rights and obligations to the three original Parties to the Treaty.

178. Timerbiev, R.M. (ed.), OON i podderžanie meždunarodnogo mira (The United Nations and the maintenance of international peace). Moscow, Izdatel´stvo Meždunarodnye Otnošenija, 1973.

The book analyses the attitudes of the Soviet Union and other socialist countries working to strengthen the prestige of the United Nations as an effective instrument for joint actions of States to maintain peace and security and deal with such problems as the non-proliferation of nuclear weapons, demilitarization of the sea bed and ocean floor, banning chemical and biological weapons, and nuclear test ban.